Shrimp Tales 2

Shrimp Tales 2

The Women of Shrimping

Rudy H. Garcia
Pat McGrath Avery

Red Engine Press
Fort Smith, Arkansas

Copyright © 2024 Rudy H. Garcia and Pat McGrath Avery

ALL RIGHTS RESERVED. No part of this book may be reproduced or transmitted in any form or by any means, electronic or mechanical, including photocopying, recording, or by any information storage and retrieval system (except by a reviewer or commentator who may quote brief passages in a printed or on-line review) without permission of the publisher.

Edited by: Rita Garcia and Christopher Avery

Cover Art by Risa E. Garcia
Cover Design by Joyce Faulkner

Library of Congress Control Number: 2024944158

ISBN: 979-8-9895620-3-9 (softcover)

DEDICATION

This book of real stories is dedicated to the hard-working women of the South Texas shrimping industry.

Contents

INTRODUCTION	vii
AMAZING WOMEN by the SEA	1
ENVIRONMENTAL IMPORTANCE of SHRIMP	7
BAYSIDE NET & TWINE	8
THE NET MAKERS	10
DOÑA ROSITA BODDEN	14
MARIANELLA (MANE) BODDEN	20
DEYANN BOUDREAUX	28
EMMA CANTU	35
PILAR CANTU	37
MARCELLA CASANOVA	60
MARIA LUISA CHAVEZ	67
TRINE & INEZ CUEVAS	71
BEATRICE FLOYD HOLLAND	76
YOLANDA CANTU GALVAN	80
RITA ALANIZ GARCIA & EULOGIA VILLAREAL ALANIZ	90
CONNIE GARZA	102
JUANITA GONZALES	107
ROSA BODDEN GONZALES	112
ANDREA HANCE	119

THE HOLLAND FAMILIES	120
PENNY BOUDREAUX LOUPE & KALEI BOUDREAUX	125
LAURA PICARIELLO	129
IDA GONZALEZ RIVERA	131
ZELDA SIERRA	134
THE QUIÑONES FAMILY	136
LUPITA VILLARREAL	156
HANDS	165

INTRODUCTION

...It takes a village...Glue...Community...

These concepts kept running through our minds as we contemplated the role of women in the shrimping industry. From wives at home raising children to women in support industries managing company offices, they stand out in every way.

It takes a village is a famous African proverb about raising children. It has been used by author Hillary Clinton in her recent book by the same name.

Glue is defined as any adhesive that is applied to hold materials together. In all our interviews and research, we found this to be an accurate description of women's role within the shrimping industry. They held the home and the towns together, they worked in support industries critical to the success of shrimping and they kept track of each boat's catch, earnings, repairs, etc.

Community... Women forged strong community ties and sustained them through the thick and thin years of the shrimping industry.

When previously interviewing the shrimpers for *Shrimp Tales*, the initial book on shrimping in Port Isabel and Brownsville, we quickly discovered that they flourished not only because the shrimp were plentiful but also because the entire community was involved - men, women and children. All played an important role in building the dynamic industry that became the shrimping capital of the world.

Reflecting on the importance of community, we realized that it truly does take a village to prosper, and that Port Isabel is a shining example of the people working toward common goals.

From shrimpers to net makers and diesel mechanics, from fish houses to offices and home fronts, women played an equal, but different, role in building and organizing the flourishing industry.

Unfortunately, the importance of women's contributions has not been researched and recognized in any publication we could find. The men who fished all spoke of the importance of, and admiration for, the women in their lives. Whatever level of success and accomplishments they have achieved in the shrimping industry, as well as in life, as husbands, fathers, and respected community members is largely due to the support and counsel of their women.

Tony Reisinger has spent his career in the coastal fisheries field, the last thirty years of which he's served as Sea Grant's Extension Agent in Cameron County. Most if not all shrimpers up and down the Texas coast know Tony and are familiar with his efforts to help keep the industry in compliance with the many governmental regulations When we approached him about interest and desire in writing a book exploring the contributions of women in the industry, his enthusiastic response pleased us. "I've met many women over the years who played significant roles and their stories need to be heard."

Our goal with this second book about the Texas shrimping history is to highlight the women's diverse roles and to present an accurate picture of the successes they achieved and challenges they met. It was not, and still is not an easy life. Managing the difficult task of kissing their husbands farewell, after a parting heart felt, with that loving embrace. Presenting for their husbands and children a strong secure looking face on the outside, holding back tears. While their bosomed hearts are throbbing with pain on the inside. Knowing good and well, that the just now untethered embrace may be their last. Shrimper wives live with this dread every day of their lives.

They live with the real thought and possibility that once their husbands, clear the rocky jetties... steer north and sail out of sight...they may never see them, talk to them, or hold them again. They know this to be true because all they must do, is to turn and look at the statue of the Christ Jesus, right there at the jetties' cove, with his outstretched arms, as he bids farewell and welcome to all sea voyaging mariners. At the base of the Cristo de los Pescadores statue, they have read and know the names of many of the husbands, fathers and sons listed and memorialized there. They too kissed their wives farewell. Except for them, the farewell kiss turned out to be a final goodbye.

It is difficult, put mildly, to be a lone parent for months at a time with husbands away at sea. Having to be both parents to children, to keep the community together, to encourage each other while maintaining a common bond of sisterhood. Having to be always ready at the sound of a siren to drop everything and head to the fish houses to process a big catch of shrimp, so that the men can ready their boats once again filled with fuel, ice, groceries and other supplies. So, these are the soulmate husbands chosen by love and fate, these are the men they will eternally adore. These are the special companions they will devote their daily lives to nurturing along with their families. These women will treasure every moment and hope that they possibly get to chat on the radio to hear that voice that gives them the strength to push forward. They may even chat with the men that their daughters will choose to love and marry someday when their time comes to be a shrimper's wife.

Again, the cycle continues... the shrimper's wife will once again kiss, bless, pray and say good-bye to her shrimper husband, keep back her tears so that her husband does not see. So that her children do not see her inner pain. Radiating with love so her husband sees only her strength outside and in so that her children see the same, always a strong mother...their rock. A mother who they know will pull no nonsense double duty. A mother who will keep them safe. A mother who will make certain that they grow as playful, cheerful children, as children are supposed to, always appreciating life. Realizing that it's tough every time they wave good-bye; always adoring the dad whose tired body endures a toll with the challenging struggles of a life at sea. The husband who will also stay strong, hug them tightly, hesitantly turn away and proudly board his shrimp boat. He will cut loose the mooring ropes and cast off. He will coil, uncoil his Cabo ropes, proceed to check and recheck his riggings and hang his nets ready. He will set his mind to the task at hand for another shrimping trip. He will know that he can now focus on his job. Because although he knows and feels his wife's worry, he appreciates her showing her strength, her love of him and for fulfilling her wife and motherly duties, of a shrimper's wife. He understands all her sacrifices and loves her endlessly. Time now to sail off. Sail off north, south, east and west. He will fish now. He will drop his nets and drag the ocean floor for crustacean gold, found in great abundance at the bottom of the Gulf of Mexico.

2

AMAZING WOMEN by the SEA

We heard many stories of women who spent their lifetimes in the business. Several women we interviewed spoke highly of Yolanda Galloway, who recently passed away from Covid. Yolanda began working as a bookkeeper in the industry right out of high school and when she was still a teenager. Over the years, she learned and with experience, gained valuable knowledge relating to all aspects of running and operating the business office part of shrimping. Each individual boat is a corporation to itself. Each has its` own set of books. Each has its own bank account.

The company bookkeeper is a position of great trust to the boat owner. Unlike an independent accountant who the boat owner hires at the end of the tax year to conduct the audit, analyze and advise the company on the amount of federal income taxes owed and need to be paid during tax season. The bookkeeper has a daily account of revenue and expenditures. They need to be able to go to the ledger and inform the owner at a moment's notice of all expenses and balances concerning the boat.

Yolanda became so skilled at her job that oftentimes bookkeepers working for other shrimp boat companies would call her for advice on matters having to do with boat bookkeeping. Over the years, she mentored many fellow office workers. Yolanda, married Jimmy Galloway, a shrimper, boat owner, and operator. This marital union gave Yolanda, extensive knowledge of operations regarding shrimp boats. She learned the hiring of the crew, the work involved with the dock workers. She also became very familiar with the daily market prices of shrimp. The price of shrimp, like all other commodity trading, changes daily. Both she and her husband monitored the up and down price fluctuations for shrimp. This helped them determine when to sell their shrimp and when to hold on to it.

Wilma Anderson served many years as the Executive Director for the Texas Shrimp Association, a position now held by Andrea Hance. She fought hard for industry rights and traveled extensively. According to several people we interviewed, Wilma knew everyone in Washington D.C. and was skilled in working and negotiating with them. Since Texas shrimpers and all other shrimping states, for that matter, do not have the financial resources available to them to hire lobbyist to wine and dine Washington fat cats, it's up to the shrimping states Executive Directors to lobby for their industry. As the saying says, "money talks" and as it is well known. Washington politicians, mostly, only really listen and act on an industry's behavior, if you visit them with money bags filled with money. As stated earlier in this section, each shrimp boat is its own corporation. And they barely earn enough money to keep themselves afloat and operate from one shrimp season to the next. After meeting all the many operating expenses. There is just not much money left over to put in the pockets of the self-serving, "you scratch my back and I'll scratch you back" politicians. The simple fact is that the little money left over for shrimpers after the season is used to feed and support their families. Even though they lost some major battles, those they won during Wilma's tenure were due in large part to her extorts.

The Executive Director position can be a thankless one and is filled with making the shrimpers' view known on government regulation issues. It seems apparent that with every year that passes, more and more government regulations are imposed on shrimpers. Apart from closing the Texas coast to shrimping, two hundred miles into the Gulf of Mexico from March to mid-July to allow the shrimp to spawn and grow to market size. Virtually all other regulations work against shrimpers and their maximized catch potential. Their nets are required to have an escape method for turtles (TEDs – turtle excluder devices), and an escape route for fish by catch. These executer devices are good and needed for the preservation of the species but it's bad for the shrimper's bottom line. Shrimpers were targeted as the major reason for the decline of the sea turtle population in the Gulf of Mexico. Some say the biased studies against shrimpers as being the cause of the dwindling turtle population was stacked against shrimpers from the get-go. That battle was won and decided in favor of sea turtles and their environmentalists, way before research studies were conducted and submitted to the government. The studies and findings submitted, presented and testified to congressional committees by researchers was a mere formality.

Shrimpers are friends of the turtle's friends. If you ask them how many sea turtles, they brought up in their nets while shrimping before TEDS, they will tell you the number was few to none. Fortunately, out of the few, almost all of them were still alive and they respectfully returned them back into the sea. Wilma Anderson was also co-owner of several boats over her tenure.

Laura Picarelli, Marine Fisheries Specialist at Texas A&M's Sea Grant Program, talked about the graying of the industry. Most involved in shrimping have been there for years and most young people, unlike their fathers and grandfathers before them, are not interested in entering the field. The Young Fishermen's Development Grant Program was established by Congress in December of 2020 to support training, education and technical assistance to young commercial fishermen. The program was administered by the National Sea Grant office.

The dwindling number of younger people or following generations not willing or interested in pursuing careers in the business of owning and operating a shrimp boat may be attributed to their very own fathers.

Shrimping is a very physically demanding and dangerous job. There are endless injury risks while working on board a shrimp boat. Boats and crew members are the mercy of mother nature with all her many weather changes and conditions. She can whip up an unexpected sudden squall or storm that can easily disable and damage the shrimp boat. She will relentlessly pound your boat with her mighty waves until she breaks it to pieces. She can lance a thundering lightning bolt at you striking you dead or cause a fire. An angry wave may slap you overboard during a rough night of high seas. If that happens. The odds that you will ever be seen or heard of again are never good? The powerful winch may grab you with its steel cables crushing you to death. You may get tangled with ropes pulling overboard with the nets. Get struck on the head with one of the many heavy iron and steel parts constantly moving back and forth on deck.

Keep in mind that a shrimp boat is a relatively small vessel out in the open sea. They average seventy to eighty feet in length. Putting them at the mercy of colossal seas or monstrous tempest storms. For these reasons captains' seamanship, skills and experiences are most important for the crew's safety. Despite a captain's many skills as a mariner who may have survived many storms though, the list of ways injury or death may occur on these boats is virtually endless.

It may be a supposition morbid analysis of the dangers of shrimping, but all you must do in putting all these risks of the job into perspective is to go Isla Blanca Park at the south end of Brazos Island (Padre Island), next to the jetties of Brazos de Santiago Pass. There you will see the statue of the Christ Jesus with his outstretched arms in blessed welcome and departure. At the base of the granite foundation where Jesus stands, memorialized are the lives of all the shrimpers from Port Isabel and Brownsville who have died at sea. A bronze plaque with their name, as well as the shrimp boat they were working on, serves as a testimonial of their fate as shrimpers.

Unfortunately, due to all the hazards, the worry families live with daily when their loved ones are shrimping is trying to say the least. All these factors may be reasons for the decline in the younger generation seeking career employment in other fields instead of shrimping. For at least three generations, fathers and mothers have been telling their sons "Stay in school study hard, get a good education, go to college, get the kind of job that will keep you at home with your wife and children. This way, you can be by your wife's side when your children are born. Be there to tell the nurse what the name of your newborn son or daughter shall be. So that the nurse may type the name out, wrap it around their tiny wrist for all the world to see. Be there to bring both your wife and baby home from the hospital. Be there to celebrate your children's birthdays, first day of school, dance recitals, little league baseball games, football games, band performances, and all the many other important growing up moments, missed out on while out at sea shrimping.

Many sons have indeed worked as shrimper deck hands. They have experienced the work firsthand. The exposure to the job with all its challenges may very well have been an influencing motive to stay in school, get an education and work at something else other than shrimping.

It's a consensus among those in the business, that government regulations, apathetic elected state and federal politicians, the high costs of outfitting, operating, maintaining, a shrimp boat, imported cheap farm raised shrimp, coupled with the reality that most of their heirs frankly do not want any part of shrimping.

All these circumstances may very well be the reason or reasons why many of the "graying" shrimpers have left or are leaving the business? Add money miss-management over the years by shrimpers as perhaps another reason for the decline in the number of shrimp boats as well. It would be wonderful for the industry if the young fishermen development grant passed by congress is successful in attracting and sustaining young shrimpers back to shrimping. That would hopefully ensure that at the very least, one more generation of shrimpers will brave the waters, to bring the wild caught shrimp the public loves to eat.

No other shrimp species in the world is better tasting than Gulf of Mexico shrimp. With proper environmental care, improved support, partnership with governmental agencies we should be able to keep the sustainability of an abundant shrimp population for harvest and delectable eating by consumers in restaurants and homes across the country.

Laura also spoke of the process differences throughout the Gulf. For example, Texas shrimpers sell through processors while Louisiana shrimpers conduct direct sales at the docks.

Another noticeable difference is the women who are currently involved in the industry. The Texas Gulf Coast is home to several women who hold influential positions, but that is not true of the Port Isabel and Brownsville market. Few are known such as Andrea Hance, who is the executive director of the Texas Shrimp Association and co-owner and operator of two shrimp boats with her husband. Penny Boudreaux Loupe and Leonor Tower, are both owners-operators of a small fleet of boats (four boats each). Also, two or three other ladies up the Texas coast in Palacios, Galveston and Port Arthur are owners because there are not many women who own and operate shrimp boats in Texas. Shrimping remains a man's world and there is no real evidence that the status of things is changing.

Andrea Hance, executive director of the Texas Shrimp Association, echoed Laura's comments about the current state of the industry. In her position, she spends most of her time fighting, lobbying, and talking to anyone who will listen to the plight of shrimpers in Austin, Texas and Washington, D.C. {government programs and the rights of shrimpers throughout the State and Washington, D.C.

Complacency among the long-time shrimpers presents an ongoing challenge. Texas shrimpers have been regulated by government policies for so many years that its bringing them closer and closer to the brink of extinction. That they feel reluctant to surge, strong, vocal protest anymore. They have done it in the past. They have gone to Austin and even to Washington, D.C. They spoke to politicians and policy makers until they became blue in the face. Yet, it seems that every year more and more regulations drive up the cost of operating a shrimp boat making it harder and harder to make a profit. It has gotten to a point where the best they can hope for is break even.

It appears that the only elected representatives willing to sit and listen to shrimpers and their industry challenges are those that represent them in their districts. Unfortunately, sit and listen is about the only thing they do. They do not go much further beyond that.

Consequently, shrimpers have become accustomed to the current status quo. Andrea feels that twenty years of fighting and losing battles has dulled the willingness to try. For example, she explained that disaster relief funds typically never reach the commercial fishermen.

The biggest issue both women see today is the dwindling workforce in the shrimping industry and it is not because of people population. There is an abundance of people in general. It's just that young people aren't interested in this hazardous industry of work.

Coupled with the lack of young people wanting to shrimp and the reduction of temporary work visas issued by the federal government. The industry continues to diminish each year. Laura, Andrea and Ida Gonzalez Rivera, bookkeeper and office manager for Bodden-Cadell, commented that most of the visa workers have been coming for twenty or more years. They are experienced, hard-working employees that the industry needs to survive. Yet in recent years shrimp boat owners have been left with fully rigged ready to go shrimp boats tied to the dock at the beginning of the shrimping season, because they could not find enough crew members to take the boat shrimping.

One of the government rationales for reducing the number of foreign temporary work visas is that there are a lot of out of work people in the U.S. that can fill the shrimping jobs available. But again, U.S. citizens do not want to work as shrimpers. It is not that the pay and money earning potential is not good. Shrimping crew members can earn some very good paydays. People here in the U.S. just do not want to do this perilous work on shrimp boats and stay at sea away from civilization for months at a time.

After the gulf oil spill, Texas is the only state that hasn't yet distributed the Restore Act relief funds. Likewise, the federal government allocated eight billion dollars to aid the commercial fishing industry. Ten years later, the funds remain untouched. Unbelievable how unfair this is to continue to hinder the much ailing shrimping industry.

The state of Texas does not issue new vessel licenses. To buy a new boat, one must be decommissioned. All these factors continue to threaten the shrimping industry and make it a grave situation altogether.

3

Environmental Importance of Shrimp

Deyaun Boudreaux brought many shrimp facts to our attention.

The Gulf of Mexico is America's richest fishery. Shrimp are the keystone of the Gulf's marine life. Because shrimp are one hundred percent nursery dependent, the water quality must be sustained. If the shrimp can thrive, so can every species of the marine food chain.

The Gulf is home to three species of shrimp - brown, pink and white. The brown shrimp is the most valuable and is the most prolific. The pink shrimp nursery is in the Florida Keys and the Intercoastal Waterway. They prefer the clearer water and whiter sand. The pink shrimp have a small nursery in the Laguna Madre on the San Padre Island side.

The white shrimp nurseries are in the mouth of the Rio Grande River and the Arroyo Colorado River. All rivers in Texas have an estuarine environment, that is an area where the fresh water source meets the ocean. The two rivers' estuaries are salt-water driven, meaning the salty sea water mixes with the fresh water further up the mouth of the river.

Louisiana estuaries are important to shrimp, but they are river driven, not salt-water driven. The brown shrimp nursery is in the Laguna Madre. Although they have different dependencies, the health of the shrimp determines the health of everything in the marine food chain.

Another interesting fact we learned is that in Texas, resources belong with the people rather than with the state. This dates to the state's history of being part of Spain. In most Gulf states, the fishing boundary was only three miles, but in Texas it was twelve. This also is inherited Latin law. When the 200-mile limit was introduced, Deyaun fought against it and lost. The law was enacted to protect the Texas shrimp from overfishing, but many thought it put Texas shrimpers at a disadvantage. Today many Texas shrimpers fish the Louisiana or Florida waters.

4

BAYSIDE NET & TWINE

Research for a book always contains unexpected gifts. While one is looking for specific information, the resulting tentacles often reach into new and unexpected places. That has happened to us on more than one occasion.

On a particular piece of research, we interviewed four ladies who worked at *Bayside Net & Twine* in Laguna Heights. One of the ladies, Emma Cantu, worked within the industry for forty-four years. We hoped to find photographs and information on the net making company and its sister companies. While we found what we were searching for, we also found a major player in the Rio Grande Valley shrimping history.

That man, Will Hardee, was born into a shrimping family and started his career in Florida in the 1930s. The son of Italian immigrants, he learned English and the shrimping business at an early age. He built his first fleet, opened related businesses and became active in civic and community organizations. He married Elnora Lang, and they had a daughter, Marjorie, before moving his entire operation to Brownsville in 1950. During his tenure, he manufactured shrimp boats, owned a fuel and ice shop, and built his fleet to more than thirty boats. He never retired and worked until his death in 1987.

His daughter, Marjorie, married Marvin Conner who joined the family business.

Will's achievements and industry positions are numerous, and he was awarded Maritime Man of the Year for his work in the Brownsville and Port Isabel area.

Dean Conner, grandson of Will, dug up photographs and the information on Will. We talked about *Bayside Net & Twine* and the people who worked there.

Will Hardee — Dean Conner (Will's grandson)

A timeline of the Hardee's family business:

1952	*Sea Garden* was founded.
1955	*Valley Ice and Fuel* is formed.
1965	*Bayside Net & Twine* is purchased.
1970	*Southern Ship Building* is dissolved.
1972	The McAllen store is closed.
1975	*Harlingen Industrial* is bought and renamed *Sea Garden*.
1988	*Valley Ice and Fuel* is sold.
1996	*Sea Garden* buys *Royal Inc.*, a metal building supplier.
1998	*Sea Garden* spins off *Royal Metal Building*. Hardee's grandchildren, Bill Conner, Dean Conner and Pat Pace, Beth Conner's husband, are company principals.
2002	*Bayside Net & Twine* equipment is sold, and the company is dissolved.

5

THE NET MAKERS

L to R: Emma Cantu, Pilar Cantu, Maria Luisa Chávez, Juanita Gonzalez

Even after interviewing four women who spent their careers as net makers, we find it difficult to present an accurate picture of the intricate net making process.

Imagine two hundred spools of twine on the back rack and two hundred bobbins (not your sewing machine variety, but each about eight-to-ten inches in diameter). In front of the machines are rows of women tending and supervising the machines. The women stand all their eight-hour shifts. They get a ten-minute break in the morning, a thirty-minute lunch, and a ten-minute break in the afternoon. They tie new bobbins and constantly look for flaws in the process.

After the net was made, it was dipped in a solution of isopropanol to tighten and strengthen it. The standard net was two hundred meshes wide and three thousand meshes long weighing two hundred fifty pounds or more depending on the size of the twine. The twine ranged in thickness from a number nine to sixty, which was a little smaller than a pen. In the early days, twine was made of cotton and a synthetic material. Later the twine became one hundred percent nylon; it was lighter and stronger.

The machines also ran the netting for the chafing gear, which goes over the netting bag after it is raised from the water. In addition to shrimp, the bag contains many fish and other sea species, which attract the ever-hungry sharks. The chafing gear protects the contents of the bag. It is constructed of a heavier twine. Then the twine goes through a solution to tighten the knots before it heads for inspection.

Sometimes during the inspection process, the machines that stretched the netting out to tighten the ties would break down, as is a common occurrence with industrial machines or all machines for that matter. The cables would snap and break. Luckily, there were no serious injuries because there were always people working around her to help. Everyone was aware of the danger. Most of the injuries reported by the ladies were on their fingers, as they spun the twine.

Pilar Cantu remembered the stress on her hands. "It was very dangerous. The twine was strong." She once caught her finger in a bobbin. Emma told us, "That was before the days of OSHA and emergency shut-offs, so I took her to the doctor right away." Although she was fine, Pilar said she lost a piece of flesh. Neither she nor the other women believed the work caused any permanent damage to their hands. The stress was in the possibility of injury. "It was important to be cautious all the time the machines were running." Chávez also suffered an injury to a finger when she was lifting a net for inspection. Her position as an inspector involved stretching the netting to tighten the knots, finding flaws and repairing them. If the flaws were minor, she could easily fix them. If they were bigger, she would have to cut another piece of the netting to repair and sew it into the netting.

Bayside Net & Twine employed twenty-one people - ten women and eleven men. Each woman spoke of mutual respect for each other's jobs. They worked eight-hour shifts Monday through Friday with two ten-minute breaks. The plant closed on weekends.

"We were a small community, and we all knew each other," Pilar stated. "I never experienced any disrespect from the men I worked with."

"We shipped nets up and down the Gulf Coast. Our nets were so well made that they were always in demand," Emma said. All four women took pride in their contribution to the industry and agreed they were happy with their career choices.

Juanita Gonzalez started working at *Bayside Net & Twine* in 1963, a short time after she was married. Her father, Cosme Garza also worked there, he would prepare and deliver the isopropanol liquid and take it to each machine, as well as delivering the twine upstairs to each station.

Emma didn't know anything about the shrimping or net making industry until she started at *Bayside Net & Twine* in 1968. She lived in Brownsville, Texas, and came to Port Isabel, after marrying her husband, Isaac Cantu. Isaac was born and raised in Port Isabel and is very familiar with shrimping. In fact, he worked as a foreman for *Marine Mart*, a shrimp boat repair railway and shrimp boat building company owned and operated by Bill and Walter Zimmerman. After six months of working at *Bayside Net & Twine*, Emma transferred to the office where she worked as an administrative assistant and eventually managed a total of forty-four years before her retirement. Pilar started in 1964 and spent the next seventeen years there.

Maria Luisa Chávez worked there for thirteen years. She and her husband, Federico, were net makers for many years. They had a shop at their home and when she wasn't working for *Bayside Net & Twine*, she helped him.

All expressed their admiration for women married to shrimpers. It was a lonely life. Not only did they assume all the responsibility for the home, but they had to face it alone for months on end.

"One of my daughters, Yolanda, married shrimper Johnny Galvan," said Pilar.

His father was a shrimper before him and so were his brothers. They all went shrimping during the summers with their father. After high school Johnny decided he was going to be a shrimper. A few years later he realized his dream. A dream most young shrimpers wish for when they start shrimping. Their first wish is to become a rig man, second is to become a captain and third is to become a captain and owner-operator of their very own shrimp boat.

Pilar got to see her daughter's loneliness. The loneliness all young shrimper wives and mothers experience. They are left alone without the warmth and comfort of a husband for weeks, sometimes months at a time. They have children to tend to, care for and love. These welcome motherly duties keep them occupied during the day. But once the children are put to bed they retire to their bed.

That is when they deal with loneliness in solitude. The endless thoughts and yearning for their husband's touch, caress and loving words. These Feelings and longings are common to all shrimper wives. Yet personally unique to each one of them. For everyone's mind has their own unique introspections, feelings, wants, needs and desires. They lay in bed alone in an isolated world, a void that can only be filled after the presence of their husbands returning home from the sea. Most faithfully turn to prayer and solace from a higher power and petitions to the Virgin Mary, for the safe return of their husbands, and fathers.

"I am grateful for all the women who remained faithful during the lonely times," Pilar said.

The company, opened by Martin and Firpo Tower, was purchased by Will Hardee in 1965 and remained in business until its closure in 2002. After *Bayside Net & Twine* closed, Mr. Rogelio Salinas opened his own net making and repair shop until his retirement. His reputation as a master net maker preceded him. Consequently, he generated enough work to make a good living and support his family.

6

Doña Rosita Bodden

    Before coming to Port Isabel in 1960, Rosita lived in Ciudad del Carmen, Campeche Mexico. She worked with her parents at their taco stand and another space where they sold clothing, blankets, tablecloths and other hand-crafted items.

    Whitman Bodden, Sr., who later became her husband, was a merchant seaman. He worked for a company that transported shrimp from Mexico to the United States. Campeche has always been a large exporter of wild caught shrimp to the U.S.

During the 1950s and up until the 1970s Port Isabel shrimpers fished the Bay of Campeche during the Texas off season. Those trips were long and adventurous. Every shrimper you talk to that fished Campeche has interesting stories to tell about fishing down in Campeche. They also have stories that they will take with them to the grave.

It was during one of Whitman's shore leaves when he meant Rosita for the first time. Like all cities in Mexico, the marketplace is the hub of social activity during the day. It is the place where residents go to buy and sell their daily goods. It is also the place for tourists to visit, observe and join in with the local culture.

One day as he walked through the market, he stopped at Rosita's clothing stand to browse. Besides the shirts and other items for sell, he happened upon a beautiful señorita Campechana (maiden from the Mexican State of Campeche), who was operating the store.

Her enchanting beauty charmed him. He bought a shirt, not because he needed it, but because he wanted to make a connection with the pretty girl working the stand. They had the normal customer=vendor exchange and that was that for the day. As Whitman walked away from Rosita's stand, he was stung by the love bug. He spent the remainder of his shore day walking around dreamy eyed, mesmerized by Rosita's alluring person. Ixchel, the Mayan Goddess of Love and Beauty had graced her.

Weeks later, on a return trip to Ciudad del Carmen for another load of shrimp, he was drawn once again to the market. He wanted to see Rosita. He found her tending the family business like she did every day. He bought another shirt. He attempted to engage in some small talk with her but Rosita didn't speak English and he didn't speak Spanish. Nonetheless the exchange of courtesies was pleasant. He left the market feeling like he maybe, hopefully, made a good impression on her.

A few more weeks passed. Once again Whitman was in Campeche. This time he didn't go to Rosita's workplace like before. He waited in the town plaza across the street from the market. He sat on a bench that gave him a good view of her and her place of work. He watched her as she went from the taco stand to the clothing stand attending to customers and interacting with the other vendors. The more he watched her, the more interested he became. At the end of the business day as Rosita walked home, he approached her He made awkward hand and word gestures to somehow communicate with her. Rosita remembered him from his previous visits to her stand.

She agreed to his clumsy request for him to walk with her. They walked a short distance, mostly in silence. The introductory chat was a bit awkward to both as Rosita recalls. The only words she remembers that Whitman verbalized during that first walk together that she understood were, "Me gustas (I like you)." Hearing him say this, Rosita thought him to be a bit bold with his choice of words. She of course didn't return the compliment. She knew better than to reciprocate in-kind. Working at the market, she was used to hearing men, young and old, use this kind of flirting towards her. She never took any of them seriously.

She didn't know at the time that Whitman's heart had already been won. Besides letting her know that he liked her, not much happened during the short walk. Whitman felt he had made a favorable impression.

He returned the next day at closing time and again they walked and talked. They communicated as best as they could exchanging words in English and Spanish. The words may have been foreign to them. But the social interaction was not. The looks, the smiles, the voice tones, the mannerisms, amplified the universal mutual fondness when two people feel a special connection to each other.

Whitman returned time and time again. He wooed her with fumbling words. Rosita reciprocated by being nice. She felt he was sincere with his intentions towards her.

The courtship lasted three years. Whitman proposed several times over the course of those three years before Rosita agreed to marry him. They had the traditional Catholic wedding.

Whitman continued to sail back and forth from Ciudad del Carmen to Port Isabel transporting shrimp. Another three years passed before they were able to migrate to the U.S. to start a new life.

Port Isabel was going to be the place of a new beginning for them. By that time, they had three children. They sailed for three days and nights across the Bay of Campeche and the Gulf of Mexico on board a shrimp boat. Whitman had purchased a property with a small house in what is known today as Laguna Heights. Before that, it was called Bayside, a small colonia outside of Port Isabel.

Within days of arriving in Port Isabel, Whitman got a job on a shrimp boat. He went shrimping, leaving Rosita and the children alone without knowing anyone in their new community. Rosita spent her days caring for the children waiting for Whitman to return. Bayside (Laguna Heights) was an unincorporated rural community. The streets were unpaved, no streetlights, poor drainage, and it was backed up against wild, empty ranch land.

Whenever it rained the streets flooded, making them impassable by car. The children had to walk through the mud to the highway to get on the school bus. Rosita did not complain. She followed and honored her husband.

She was now a shrimper wife and she adapted. She did what she needed to do. She focused on raising and educating her children. She also became involved in her parish church.

It didn't take her long to become a social activist for her community. Seeing the poor living conditions in Laguna Heights, Rosita decided something needed to be done. They lacked basic infrastructure such as paved streets, drainage, sewer service, streetlights, police patrols, fire protection and trash pickup.

Colonias in the Rio Grande Valley fall under the jurisdiction of county government. Consequently, all the afore-mentioned services that are taken for granted in cities, were dealt with indifference and gross negligence by the County Judge and commissioners court of the time. Colonias were treated with detached isolationism both by cities and elected county officials. Seeing this insensitivity, Rosita became an advocate for improved living conditions. Using a soft but obvious approach, she visited the County Commissioner to petition for better county services in Laguna Heights.

She also advocated for better educational services for the children of the Laguna Madre area. She became an activist for improved living conditions in Laguna Heights. She became a champion and promoter in establishing a safe haven for the children of the Laguna Madre to gather after school and weekends. She lobbied and was successful in uniting the cities of South Padre Island, Port Isabel, Laguna Vista, the Point Isabel School District and the United Way in funding, charting and bringing a Boys and Girls Club for the Laguna Madre Youth.

She got involved with religious charitable work in her church parish, Our Lady Star of the Sea. Encouraged by an old feisty, fearless Missionary Oblate priest, the Reverend Father Joseph O'Brien, she joined Valley Inter-Faith, an organization made up of faith and community leaders. Their mission was to train and develop grass roots community leaders, empowering them to speak up for and let their voices be heard at local city halls, school boards, county courts and the state capitol of Texas.

As it turned out Rosita, a diminutive figure (less than five feet tall) with virtually no English language at her command, became a giant to Valley Inter Faith's cause in reforming and improving living, health and educational conditions for the less fortunate throughout Texas.

The once quiet, shy, reserved, obedient, immigrant housewife from Ciudad del Carmen, Campeche, Mexico, with small children at home became a disquieting leader, a public servant and an advocate for equal rights. Though she never spoke with a loud, angry voice, she was unnerving and unrelenting. She summoned her inner strength, guided by the Holy Spirit, making sure she and others like her were not going to be excluded from having their say in front of decision-making government officials, who for too many years callously ignored the poor, neglected, voiceless.

The tiny soft-spoken Mayan warrior often needed a step stool to stand on, to be seen and heard from behind the speaker podiums. There were times when elected government officials refused to meet with her and her group. They made up flimsy excuses as to why they couldn't meet with them to hear their concerns and demands.

The evasive excuses did not deter Rosita. She would simply wait outside of their offices for them to come out. She did not possess a formal education beyond the fifth grade, nor was she a trained orator. There were many highly trained and educated individuals within the Valley Inter-Faith organization.

Yet for some reason, she was frequently the one who was chosen to stand and speak before city and governmental panels to express their concerns. She had a certain eloquence and confident presence about her. She had learned from Father Joe that if she had right and God at her side, she had nothing to fear. Her persistence along with the organizational efforts of Valley Inter-Faith resulted in the improvement of many much-needed services for the poor. They got educational reform, indigent health care, community clinics, better water, sewer and drainage services for colonias.

She also got involved in fighting against TEDS (turtle excluder devices) on Gulf trawling shrimp boats, as well the closure of the two-hundred-mile limit for shrimping during the off season. That unfortunately was a fight they did not win. Her legacy as well as the covenant pledge shrimper wives make to their husbands and families is what has made Port Isabel, and other shrimping towns prosperous and vibrant communities.

Rosita (center)

7

MARIANELLA (MANE) BODDEN

"I live with loneliness. I envy a lot of friends of mine. I know I shouldn't and ask God for forgiveness. But for some reason only the Lord knows, I've been alone most of my life. My kids help me, but I still get lonely. I still get sad and miss him. I have his picture and talk to him often."

Mane still misses her husband, Whitman William Bodden. She lost him to the turbulent waters of the Gulf of Mexico in 2009.

She grew up in Port Isabel. Her grandparents and parents owned grocery stores. Her maternal grandfather and father, Benito Ochoa, Sr. and Benito Ochoa Jr., also owned a shrimp boat many years ago. Her father was a shrimper for a while. Mane was a baby and too young to remember but her mother, Maria, told her the story.

Her father was out shrimping when he and his crew were caught in a storm. The storm battered the boat so that it became disabled in the water. It started to take on water. It was sinking. Her father was able to send a "mayday" distress radio call to the Coast Guard. They were rescued just as the boat was about to go under. That was the end of her father's shrimping career. His wife decided that he was not going shrimping again. He went into the grocery store business with his father instead.

The store, Ochoa's Grocery, was in the middle of Mexiquito. There were other stores that sold groceries in Mexiquito, but they were smaller mom and pop stores that mostly sold bread, soda pop and candy. The Ochoa's catered to families who shopped with carts. The husband, wife and kids came once a week and filled the cart with five-pound sacks of flour, beans, and potatoes, pounds of sugar, coffee, vegetables and can goods. Ochoa's also had a meat market. Once a week, the mother went with the husband for their weekly groceries but did not return to the store for the rest of the week. The meat was bought daily. Most Mexiquito homes had refrigerators, but they did not keep meat well.

Every day one of the boys in the family, usually the oldest or the oldest plus a more astute younger brother would go to Ochoa's to buy the pound of meat for the day. It was always only one pound per day. Most families in Mexiquito were large, anywhere from six to ten or twelve. The size of the family didn't change the weight of the meat bought for the day. It was always going to be one pound regardless.

The store also sold groceries to many shrimpers. They were the biggest customers. Shrimpers spent a lot of money at his store. Because of this Don Benito allowed the wives to take groceries on credit while the husbands were out fishing. When the boats came in and the men got paid, they went back to Don Benito and settled the account.

"My dad would sometimes take my sister and me in the VW van to the docks when he delivered groceries to the boats. I went to school with Whitman's brother. We got married when I was seventeen. He was eighteen," Mane said.

Whitman William Bodden was born in Campeche, Mexico. The Boddens were originally from Honduras. His father was a merchant mariner. His job brought him to the Port of Brownsville, delivering supplies. After several trips to Brownsville, the older Bodden saw there was potential for him as a shrimper. He took the risk and changed jobs from merchant mariner to shrimper. The change of jobs paid off. He earned enough money to buy a home, return to Campeche and bring his wife and three children. They settled in Laguna Heights.

After relocating his family, making sure they were well situated, he went back out shrimping. His wife Rosita and the children started a new life in Port Isabel.

Young Whitman started shrimping as a header with his dad as a young boy. By that time his father had prospered. At one time Mr. Bodden owned four boats. After working as a header for a few years Whitman moved up to rig man. On his first trip as a rig man, he had his first hard test at sea. They got caught in a tropical storm. It was the most frightening experience he had yet experienced. Although they usually took safe harbor in the closest port, captains sometimes chose to outrun the storm and make it home. He didn't, Whitman later told Mare, "The waves were so high that they picked us up and dropped us back down over and over like nothing. Huge waves kept coming over the bow and the cabin. Sometimes the boat tilted so far to one side and then the other that I thought we were going to flip over. I have never prayed so hard in my life."

A few years after that, Whitman moved to a bigger boat as a captain. He lived through many tempest storms out at sea. The Gulf of Mexico, like all large bodies of water, is always unpredictable. Mariners never know when a sudden storm or squall will develop and come churning at you. Cold fronts can be just as dangerous. During the winter months, strong, powerful winds out of the north regularly make it to the Gulf of Mexico. These waves can be as big and menacing as tropical storms.

"He was smart," Mane said. "He learned how to repair almost any kind of mechanical breakdown. He did most of his repairs. That way he could stay out longer, plus save money. Boat repairs cost a lot of money. He captained the *Daisy Patricia*. It was an ice boat when his father first let him captain it. Later, when all the boats started working with freezers on board, they converted her to refrigeration."

"He would leave in May for Louisiana and return in July. I was left alone with three children. When he came back, he would still be gone most of the day working on the boat getting it ready for the next trip or the shrimping season. We only got to be with him for three or four days after months-long fishing trips. When he was in port, the kids and I hung around the boat. That was the only way we could spend more time with him. He left again in July, returning after Labor Day. It wasn't as hard on me when kids were small. It was easier for me to manage them."

"Later, as they got older, their interests, friends and behaviors changed. They wanted more freedom. With that discipline issues changed. The troubles, problems and concerns got bigger, more serious. I always told him everything that happened with the kids. We always agreed on discipline. He had a deep booming voice and when he spoke, they listened to him."

"Later on, he would often go into Port Lavaca to unload and sell the shrimp. They got paid better for the shrimp over there. He always needed something for the boat. So, I packed up the kids, loaded the supplies he needed and off we went. The kids loved it. It was like a mini vacation for us. He loved it too, we got to spend time together as a family. I always tried to take kids with me. It gave him, the kids and me time to see each other and spend a few days together as a family. We took many trips like that over the years."

"His family owned four or five boats. We were part owners on one. He was the only one of the brothers who liked shrimping. His father put him in charge of repairs and supplies for all the boats. He learned about working on engines, electrical systems and mending the nets."

"The *Daisy Patricia* almost sank once. The crew was eating dinner and watching television during a rough, stormy night. The boat got hit by lightning. Everything went dark. All the electrical system was blown out, nothing worked. When Whitman went down to the engine room to turn on the generator, he found it flooded. Luckily, he got the generator to work. He had enough power for the radio to work, but not enough to start the bilge pump to pump out the water. He ran to the wheelhouse and called the Coast Guard. He gave them their coordinates and told them they were taking on lots of water. He told them his pump wasn`t working, so, he couldn`t pump the water out. They were sinking! He ordered the crew to put on their life jackets and get the life raft ready."

"Luckily for them, the Coast Guard helicopter arrived just in time. They lowered a pump down to him. He connected it and was able to pump the water out and save the boat. During the time they were waiting for the Coast Guard to arrive, he kept thinking how he didn't know how to swim. The waves were huge. He said it was one of his scariest times."

"When Whitman was fishing, we were able to talk with the use of a radio. Whitman's father owned and ran a local liquor store on South Shore Drive down by the docks. He had a radio with a tall antenna that picked up radio waves way out at sea. This is how he kept tabs on his boats. We also wrote letters to each other and sent them back and forth with other boats."

"The first week he was gone was always the hardest on me. I prayed a lot, especially at night when I was in bed alone. I prayed the rosary and asked the Virgin of Guadalupe to take care of him and to bring him back home to us safe."

"He worried about me too. He was a little jealous. There was no reason for it. He was the love of my life. Deep down inside he knew it. But that's the way he was. Nights were always the worst for me. That's when I missed him the most. It was difficult for me to sleep. The prayers helped. I would pray the rosary over and over, until I fell asleep. In the morning when I woke up, I would still have the rosary in my hands.

"He seldom made it home for Thanksgiving, but he never missed Christmas. For the most part, all the shrimpers come home for Christmas. It's a special time of year for us. Everyone has money to spend. The children get nice gifts. The fish houses and boat owners pay out Christmas bonuses. The husbands take the wives to dinner and dancing in nice, fancy restaurants on Padre Island, Brownsville and Matamoros, Mexico."

"We get a full two weeks straight as a family without interruptions from the boat. The boat rests, too. Well almost no interruptions. Every morning after breakfast, the captains must go to the boat for about an hour to pump it. Water always finds a way to get in, so it must be pumped every day. He also checks the engine room, the cabin and the decks before leaving the boat. They check all the ropes to make sure the boat is tied good and secure to the dock."

"I was the one taking the kids to school, practices and school events. I once drove to Port Lavaca to take supplies, had lunch with him, hugged and kissed him goodbye, got back in the car and drove back home in time to take my son to a baseball game. Everywhere I went, I took all the kids with me. Often, I took nieces and nephews, too."

"After many years of shrimping. Whitman decided to look for work on land. He thought he had finally gotten shrimping out of his system. By that time, the kids were all grown. He found a job as a jailer with the Sheriff's office. The Chief Jailer absolutely loved him."

Whitman was a big, wide, brawny, strong man with powerful hands and arms. His forearms were as thick or thicker than most men's leg thighs.

All those many years of pulling, lifting, heaving, and tossing heavy things around on the shrimp boat, he developed a physique ideally suited for guarding and managing inmates in a county jail. Add his booming, deep rugged, voice to the mix and the inmates under his supervision were gentle as lambs.

He worked with the Sheriff's department for two years. However, his yearning for the sea was not out of his system after all. His old sea legs began to ache for the rolling motion of the ocean. He heard they were hiring captains on utility boats to ferry supplies out to the oil rigs in the Gulf of Mexico. He applied and was hired. The Sheriff was sorry to see him go. They even offered him a promotion not to leave. But the sea was calling him. Supply boat companies absolutely love hiring local shrimpers, especially captains. These men know the Gulf of Mexico like the back of their hand. They know how to navigate on the open waters of the Gulf. It's second nature to them. They know how to read all the instrumentation of the boat with no problems. They are familiar with the areas where the oil rigs are located. They are accustomed to staying away from home for long periods of time. A month on with two weeks off is a lot better than two months out with one week off as far as they are concerned. They know how to live and manage men living in close quarters for weeks at a time.

Whitman was a perfect fit to captain a supply boat. He was a proven leader. He had many years of experience steering boats in the Gulf of Mexico and knew how to manage a crew.

"He told me that If he could do this for a couple years, we can save enough money to travel," Mane said. "I didn't want him to do it. I had gotten used to him coming home every night after work from his job as a jailer."

"I was tired of being by myself. I lived that lonely life for too many years. I didn't want to go through it all over again. Our three older children were gone. I didn't want to be by myself anymore. Especially that the kids were gone." Mare paused a few moments, her eyes got watery. "He loved the work. He loved being out on the Gulf."

"Then February 22, 2009, the saddest day of my life, he died in the Gulf of Mexico that he loved so much. He fell overboard. It still hurts to talk about it. His boat was tied to a sister boat at the dock. The company had a dispatcher shift change. The new guy sent them out during a cold front."

"They went out into a cold, windy, rough sea. One of the guys even got seasick because it was too rough."

"They were operating the lift with supplies. The big waves were rocking the boat too much. The lift line swung too far. Whitman stepped in to grab the line. A big pipe swung towards him. He couldn't get out of the way. The pipe hit him. He was knocked off the boat and into the water.

"The other crew members could see where he was in the choppy water. He was trying to stay above water but he didn`t know how to swim. They immediately began to try to pull him out. He was wearing a life jacket but was still having a hard time keeping his head out of the water. The waves were too big. They kept hitting him on the face. He was swallowing and choking on sea water."

"The captain panicked because they had little time to save him. He was afraid the propeller would hit him, so, he didn't move the boat. They kept yelling at him to hold on. They threw him a lifeline; the waves kept hitting his face. He was swallowing too much water. He got to the lifeline. His co-workers tried to pull him up. But he couldn't hold on. The waves were too big. He drowned."

"That night I was lying in bed. I felt something, it was a strange feeling I had never felt before. I felt like something was wrong. I started praying. the rosary. I fell asleep after a while. An hour or two later, my brother Benny called me with the bad news. He told me Whitman had fallen overboard and drowned. He said it happened around ten at night."

"Thinking back on that sad night, I keep thinking how I felt. Something kept telling me, something was wrong. I will never forget that feeling. It stills haunts me today."

"He wanted to be cremated but didn't want his ashes to be thrown out at sea, so we buried his remains on land."

"All those many years we were married, I felt alone a lot of the time. I'm talking about the aloneness of a wife, a woman, who misses her husband and wishes he was home with her. I`m still alone. He wasn't home when our first three kids were born. My kids help me now. They visit often. I visit with the ones who live out of town as often as I am able; but I still feel lonely. It`s been twelve years. I still get sad and miss him. I have his picture on the night stand next to my bed. I pick it up and talk to him sometimes."

Mane is proud of her family. Michelle, the oldest, went back to college and is almost finished. Willie (Whitman Lorance) has a degree in Finance and works at *La Mantia & Farias*, the biggest Budweiser distributorship in the Rio Grande Valley. Shelby works as a media specialist with Port Isabel schools. William Johnathan graduated from Texas State University in San Marcos. He is a teacher/coach and is now a coach with Point Isabel Independent School District.

When we asked Mane about how she now feels about Whitman's career, she gave an honest answer. "I do have some resentment. He always wanted to go shrimping. I wanted him to stay home. Sometimes I go to the beach for walks. I look up at the sun and sky and pray for him. It makes me feel as if he is up there looking down at us. I still ask why. Why did this happen to me? I see married couples, friends of ours that we used to hang out with. I see them at church, at school events with their grand kids, at dances or around town having a good time. I feel happy and glad for them, I love to see it, but deep inside of me. I wish Whitman and me were still a couple. It makes me sad."

8

DEYANN BOUDREAUX

The teacher who charmed a generation of Port Isabel kids transitioned to a career championing the shrimp that make their home in the Gulf of Mexico. From language teacher to environmentalist, Deyann left an indelible mark on the Valley.

Growing up with a dad who, as an engineer working around the world, proved an invaluable benefit to Deyaun's development. Living in the Bahamas, Guatemala, Vietnam and Panama exposed her to cultures totally unknown to her young students, most of whom had never been out of Cameron County, Texas.

After graduating from college in Texas in 1964, she married Ronald Boudreaux. In 1949, the Boudreaux family had moved from Morgan City, Louisiana to Texas. As part of the original Louisiana shrimpers, they came to Port Isabel and made their mark on the shrimping industry here. They were in search of better fishing grounds. A small group of them sailed south to try the fishing waters off Port Isabel and northern Mexico. The excursion paid off big time. They found more shrimp than they had imagined.

They returned to Morgan City where they belonged to a shrimp fishing operation named Twin City. They fueled their boats, packed all their belongings and relocated to Port Isabel, where they opened Twin City Co-op, a new fish house and freezer. "Would you believe Ronald's dad actually introduced us? My family owned a restaurant in Morgan City and he and his dad were customers. Then we both went to college before we met again."

Ronald continued the story. "She was in her senior year at the University of Texas in Austin. We soon started teaching. Three years later, his dad died, and Ronald took over the shrimp boats. "I'd drive around fish house row looking for him. Sure enough, I would usually find him way up in the main mast or an outrigger doing some kind of work," Deyaun remembered. "My heart would drop." Not long after, she had been married to a shrimper, Deyaun began to understand the concerns of shrimpers' wives.

Safety was the greatest worry. Wives can deal with a poor fishing trip where not many shrimps are caught, they can handle the loneliness of being left alone while the husband is away for many days and they can accept minor injuries on the job.

The one thing no wife or mother can live with is the tragic news that a husband or son was killed on the job. Worst still is being told their loved one fell overboard, and the body has not been found.

The thought of knowing that somewhere out in the vast deep waters of the Gulf of Mexico, the solitary remains of their husband or son lies alone without a marker or a memorial of their remotest, unknown resting place. Living the rest of their lives without closure.

Deyaun learned and embraced the fact that shrimping families whose fathers work for a company become part of their family as well. The boat owner, or rather the wife of the boat owner, is given the responsibility of fostering the wife and children. Shrimper wives often need a partial, advance payment on a hopefully big catch. The children need food, clothes and household bills need to be paid.

For the most part, wives are frugal and careful with their money and can make it last until the husband returns from shrimping and gets paid.

"My first teaching job had been in the Panama Canal Zone before I came back and finished college," Deyaun recalled. "Then schools superintendent Millard Caudill hired us. He was the nicest man ever, the high school is named after him, in honor of his many years of service to Point Isabel ISD."

"Did you know he was Chief of Staff to Admiral Halsey during the war?" Ronald asked. We did not. "When I started teaching, Ruben Torres was principal of the high school. I worked with his wife, Maria, on several issues including Title IX federal grants." After her teaching career, Deyaun served on the Point Isabel School Board for twelve years and was a partner in an art gallery at the Queen Isabella Inn.

After she became involved in the Vulcanus burn issue, she served eighteen years in the environmental side of shrimping, most of them as the Environmental Director of the Texas Shrimping Association.

Deyaun played a key role in forming the Gulf Coast Coalition for Public Health, which was organized to fight for clean waters in the Gulf of Mexico. She worked alongside Catholic priest Father Joseph O'Brien and the Valley Interfaith as they all fought to save the Gulf Coast from the threat of allowing the Vulcanus and Chemical Waste Management Inc., to burn PCP, DDT, and other hazardous, toxic waste residues in the water. This project would have not only killed all sea life within a forty-mile radius of the burn site but within time, all sea life in the Gulf of Mexico.

The plan was that Waste Management Inc. was to receive a three-year permit from the Environmental Protection Agency to burn chemical waste in the Gulf of Mexico.

Fortunately, some people in the news media found out about the planned agreement between the EPA and Waste Management Inc. and reported on it. Greenpeace and other environmental groups also found out about it and started the movement to "Ban the Burn." Father Joe joined the cause and brought in Valley Interfaith. Deyaun immediately followed suit in the fight against the Vulcanus. They recruited shrimper wives to join in the fight as well. They came in full force and ready to do battle.

After the news reports went out and the environmentalists started demanding answers to questions on the potential dangers and long-term hazardous results of these burns, not only on the environment but on coastal residents as well. The EPA, who at first thought it was going to be an unchallenged deal, took a step back after the environmentalists and local shrimpers began to stir the waters. They decided to hold public hearings in an effort to make it seem as if they were earnestly being conscious of the environment.

Little did Waste Management Inc. and the EPA realize or anticipate that on their first public hearing in Brownsville, TX, a troupe of angry shrimper wives led by a feisty old priest, whose flock was made up entirely of shrimpers, and Deyaun were about to inundate their hearing and give them a piece of their mind. They made it known loud and clear that they were not going to be intimidated. The strong and fearless women of the shrimping industry were not about to allow some billion-dollar waste management corporation to come to town and take away their livelihood, ruin their health and the health of their children.

As far as the wives were concerned, the men on the hearing panel were just men. The education and titles they placed on the table in front of them did not impress the shrimper women one bit. They knew how to handle men. They had plenty of experience. They had been raising boys into men all their lives.

The hearing was a disaster for the committee. They left town hoping to regroup in Louisiana and in another Gulf Coast state where they had scheduled other public hearings. But everywhere they went, the shrimper women went too. And they weren't alone.

Deyaun recalled, "We had to delve deeply into the scientific research on incineration at sea. We discovered deficiencies in their process and working with the Federal government and the state of Texas and local organizations, we defeated the project and the technology. U.S. Representative Solomon Ortiz (from Corpus Christi), with one of the coalition members, traveled to Mexico City to gain the support of the Mexican president. Mexico then joined us in our fight to save our waters."

"Waste Management had chosen the Gulf of Mexico because it was the area of least resistance to the burning," Ronald added. "It took multiple organizations and governmental entities to understand the issues and save all species in the Gulf waters. We were successful in getting legislation passed to de-designate the burn site."

After this battle was won, Deyaun was at loose ends. She wanted to continue working on environmental issues.

"If you're going to save the world, why don't you get involved with shrimping?" Ronald asked me. He was a board member of the Texas Shrimp Association then. "So, I did."

For eighteen years, she dedicated herself to environmental issues that affected shrimp and all marine life in the Gulf of Mexico. Wilma Anderson, President of the Texas Shrimp Association was the one who officially hired her as the Environmental Director of the Texas Shrimp Association.

Her focus has been on protecting the quality of water in the Gulf of Mexico and its tributaries. This has involved everything from dredging the Intercostal Waterway to protection of fresh water sources, oil spills and the Vulcanus offshore toxic incineration proposal.

"The Gulf of Mexico is the world's richest fishery, and the shrimp are the keystone to the health of everything in the marine food chain. They are one-hundred-percent nursery dependent.

Every river that runs through Texas has an estuarine environment. An estuary is an area where a freshwater river or stream meets the ocean. In estuaries, the salty ocean mixes with a freshwater river, resulting in brackish water. Louisiana estuaries are important, but they are river driven. In Texas they are salt-water driven.

The Gulf is home to three species of shrimp, brown, pink and white. The brown is the most valuable because it is the most prolific. The pink shrimp's nursery is mainly in the Florida Keys and the Intercostal Waterway. They prefer the clearer water and whiter sand. The pink shrimp have a small nursery in the Laguna Madre on the San Padre Island side. The white shrimps' nurseries are in the mouths of the Rio Grande River and the Arroyo Colorado River. The brown shrimp nursery is in the Laguna Madre. The brown is the most valuable because they are the most prolific. Although they have different dependencies, in all three species, the health of the shrimp determines the health of everything above and below them in the food chain.

"I called myself the Godmother of the Turtles when I testified before the U.S. Fisheries Commission to convince them that the shrimpers were working within and following the practices of the Endangered Species Act. We were not the source of the turtle population problem." Deyaun spoke of Ila Loetscher, the Turtle Lady, whom she knew well. "We testified together in Washington a number of times over the years."

She was the one responsible for setting up the meeting with industry specialists and politicians at both the state and federal levels.

In addition to that role, she has served on the boards of the Texas Environmental Coalition and the International Center for the Solution of Environmental Problems. She held a seat on the Gulf of Mexico Fisheries Management Council's Advisory Panel on Fisheries Habitat, has been a member of the EPA's International Border Environmental Problems Public Advisory Committee and acted as the fisheries representative to the Citizen Advisory Commission for NASA's Stennis Space Center Gulf of Mexico program.

The Office of Water Protection and Texas Parks & Wildlife do a superb job. They have been productive in protecting the Gulf for keystone species and all others. Our Texas politicians including U.S. Representative Solomon Ortiz, U.S. Representative Kika de la Garza, U.S. District Court Judge Filemon Vela, and others were all friends of the environment.

Another fight involved the 200-mile limit against shrimping when the season closed. Mexico and Cuba also instituted the 200-mile designation. That has forced our shrimpers to fish in the off- season in Louisiana and Florida waters.

The issue of imports has caused harm to U.S. fishermen and shrimpers. Most foreign shrimps are farm-raised with little or no government oversight. When the U.S. first imposed a law requiring the labeling of the origin of imports, countries would send their product to Mexico, where it would be repackaged and relabeled. They could get it into the U.S. through NAFTA. They were successful in their efforts to improve inspection of foreign shrimps.

"People want wild-caught because they know they are raised in clean water. Foreign shrimps are not raised in clean water and bring in disease. For that reason, fishermen can't use imported shrimp for bait. This is currently policed by the Texas Parks & Wildlife."

When asked how they tell the difference, Deyaun had a ready answer, "Farm-raised shrimp are dead. If they're alive, they're from Texas."

"In Texas, resources belong to the people, not the state. We get that from Latin law because we were settled by, and part of Spain, at one time."

In the 1940s, Brownsville had no shrimping business. Then the Hondurans and Estonians arrived at the same time. When World War II broke out, Germany captured Estonia and gave the men the choice to join the German army. When the Russians defeated the Germans, they did the same. By the time the Estonians came to Texas, they had served in three armies. They were brave and tough. Ester Kenon, the widow of Bill Kenon, is a descendant of the Estonians.

9

EMMA CANTU

Emma and Pilar married brothers. Emma's husband worked for *Zimco Marine*, owned and operated by Bill and Walter Zimmerman. He worked there as a foreman for thirty-eight years, in the shipbuilding part of *Zimco*. He wanted to buy his own boat, but Emma had heard too many stories about the loneliness shrimper wives endure when their husbands were out to sea for months at a time. She wanted no part of that.

They had two children, Esther, a schoolteacher who married Charlie Castillo, who happens to be Joe Castillo's brother. Charlie and Esther, like Joe and Cecilia, own a seafood restaurant and market. Their son

Isaac works as a bailiff with the State of Texas, District Courts in Brownsville.

Once three of the women at *Bayside* were simultaneously pregnant. "Marvin (Conner) jokingly told me not to drink the water." Their daughter Esther is a teacher at the Los Fresnos High School.

Dean Conner spoke highly of Emma Cantu, one of the net makers we interviewed. "She was a wonderful lady. She worked at *Bayside* and *Sea Garden Sales*. Emma had moved into the office and soon was responsible for most of the operations. My dad had a manager that either quit or was fired, I don't remember which. Emma asked, 'Who are you going to hire?' Dad immediately replied, 'You.

You're already doing the work. She stayed with us until her retirement.

Cake served at Emma's retirement party.

10

Pilar Cantu

"I wonder how I raised them..." Pilar laughed at the thought of raising six children while working a full-time job.

"I'm proud of all of them." Her smile said it all. She and her husband, Merced Cantu Jr., who was a mechanic and Korean War army veteran, worked on cars in his back yard. Merced wanted to one day own his own mechanic shop. Pilar saved her earnings from working at *Bayside Net & Twine*. After a few years of hard work and saving money, they had enough put away to purchase a property in Laguna Heights, two city blocks from *Bayside Net & Twine*. They built a small one stall auto repair shop. It was a dream come true for both. They had worked hard and now they had acquired the American dream. They owned a home and a small business. Merced was a U.S. Citizen born and raised in Port Isabel. His family had been in the U.S. for several generations. Pilar was an immigrant from Mexico. She came to the land of opportunity with the same aspirations and desires like every other immigrant has. To work hard and make a better life for herself. She brought with her a fourth-grade education, her Spanish language and the intelligence of a university graduate. "I only went to fourth grade," Pilar unapologetically admitted. "I wanted my kids to have a good education and we made that happen." Pilar and Merced made sure their children went to school every day. They made sure the children understood that their teachers were their second parents at school and that they needed to give them the same respect and mindfulness. They were expected to behave. Misbehavior was not an option. They were never to be the cause of any problems and they were to bring home report cards with high academic grades and good behavior marks.

Her oldest Leticia, is a prominent architect, is married with children and lives in Austin, Texas. Her second child, Yolanda, worked in the counseling department with Point Isabel ISD and was also a co-owner of a shrimp boat. Her third Merced Cantu III is an auto mechanic, landlord and co-owner of *Cantu's Auto Repair and Wrecker Service*. The same auto repair garage his father established when Merced the III was a young boy. The small auto garage his father started many years ago is of course much larger now with a crew of mechanics under him. The fourth, Martin, is also a landlord and business partner with Merced the III, in the auto repair and wrecker service. They also own and operate a fleet of Taxi cars.

The fifth, Raphael, is a schoolteacher and coach and her youngest, Lisa, is also a teacher.

Growing up, like most girls in Port Isabel, Pilar worked heading shrimp in the fish houses when the boats came in. When asked about her experiences there, she remembered a weigh master who flirted with her. After she filled her bucket with the shrimp heads, she would take it to him, he always managed to weigh the scales slightly in her favor.

Pilar's journey to her now self-actualized life of her golden years, was not without trials, tribulations and hardship.

She came to Port Isabel, as a fifteen-year-old young lady. Before coming to Port Isabel, she lived in a farming and ranching community on the hilly out-skirts of Linares, Mexico, in the State of Nuevo Leon. Her father Don Rafael Cuellar was a police officer. They lived a happy tranquil life on the beautiful foothills of the Grand Sierra Madre. Back then she was a senorita of fifteen, Pilar, with the help of her parents, began to put together her dowry chest and other items.

Merced was nowhere in the picture. In fact, Pilar had no inclination or thought of someday living in the United States. Her world was a world of farming and ranching in Mexico. The same as it was for the other families that worked the rural lands surrounding Linares after the Mexican revolution of 1910. Land reform and ejidos (communal commercial farming) replaced the large haciendas. Families now had their own parcels of land to work and make a living.

As is the case in all shared communities. You must have law and order. Pilar's father, Don Rafael, was a member of the small police force assigned to keep the peace. Things were going well for Pilar and her family. They had their small parcel of land, their father had a respectable position, she and her sister were going to school and looking forward to better things.

Then suddenly, everything came crumbling down around them. One night there was a disturbance in the commune. Don Rafael was summoned to his duty. He responded to the place where the fracas was taking place. Shots were fired, bullets flew in all directions. One of the bullets struck Don Rafael, killing him.

Right there and then Pilar's life was suddenly and unexpectedly shattered. The family's head of household, bread winner, their rock murdered. All was lost. Pilar's mother became a heartbroken widow, with three young girls. Pilar, Refugia and Josefina. It was time to leave. No one in the ejido (ranching commune) was going to assume the added burden of a mother with three daughters.

Don Rafael had a sister living in Port Isabel, Doña Catarina Cuellar Garcia. Upon learning of her brother's demise and the family he left behind, living in hardship. Doña Catarina traveled to Linares. She brought Pilar, sisters and mother to the Brownsville-Matamoros border. None of them had travel visas or passports. The next step was to figure out how they were going to cross over into the U.S.

Doña Catarina who was a very resourceful businesswomen rented a small room for Pilar, her mother and sisters in Matamoros, until she could figure out how she was going to bring them across. She returned to Port Isabel, to make plans and arrangements for the crossover. As it turned out Refugio, one of Pilar's sisters had a very close facial resemblance to a cousin who was living in the United States and had a green card. Doña Catarina borrowed the card and brought it with her to Matamoros. She used it to cross Refugio over.

She hired Mr. Merced Cantu Sr., who had a taxi service in Port Isabel, to drive her to Matamoros. This is where and how Pilar, first became somewhat familiar with the Port Isabel, Cantu family. Doña Catarina told Pilar's mother that she was bringing Refugio, across the international bridge with the cousin's green card. Pilar, her mother and Josefina, would be coming over by wading across the Rio Grande and its dangerously unpredictable under tow with the help of a coyote.

Doña Catarina paid the coyote in advance, a mistake they later regretted. Pilar, mother and sister were handed over to the coyote, who took them to a crossing point upriver. There he hid them in a small jacal (hut).

He told them to stay inside the hut, not to make any noise and not to go outside for anything. He would return after dark to cross them over.

They did as they were told. They had no other choice. They had no idea where they were.

Frightened and worried they huddled together in the corner of the hut and began to pray, hoping that the night would come fast and for the prompt return of the coyote.

Back in Matamoros, Doña Catarina coached the also frightened Refugia. She made her up to look as much as possible like the picture of her cousin on the green card. She told her not to talk at all when they came to the immigration inspection station on the U.S. side. She, Doña Catarina, was going to hold the green card and present it to the customs officials. She made her memorize her cousin's name and told her not to speak unless she was asked her name, to which she was going to respond Carlota, and Puerto Isabel. If she was asked anything else after that. She was to reply in Spanish "perdon no comprendo" (sorry I don't understand). It was common back than for green card holders not to speak any English at all. Custom officials were used to it.

She was also told to place and keep her hands resting gently on her lap. She was to keep her eyes looking straight forward, stay calm, no shaking of any kind and show no sign of nervousness.

Refugia did exactly as she was told. When they drove up to the customs inspection station. Doña Catarina was sitting on the back seat directly behind Mr. Cantu. Refugia was sitting on the opposite end of the back seat further away from the customs official.

Back then during the 1940s Brownsville, Texas was a mid-size town, not small but not large either. Port Isabel was small.

Automobiles were considered a luxury in this part of the world. Not many people owned one. Taxi cars were a common mode of transport.

Because of this, customs officials were familiar with most cab drivers who drove people to and from the U.S. and Mexico on a regular basis. Mr. Cantu was one of the cab drivers familiar to immigration officers at the Brownsville-Matamoros International bridge.

The inspector greeted Mr. Cantu and asked him the usual questions. Anything to declare? Mr. Cantu said no. What is your business Matamoros today? Mr. Cantu told the officer that he drove Doña Catarina over for some shopping.

The Inspector then turned his attention to Mr. Cantu's passengers. Leaning over, his head just inches' way from almost poking his head into the back seat. He looked them over for a moment, as they are trained to do, to see if he would detect any visual signs of abnormality, while at the same time asking the question that automatically rolls off their tongue as soon as a car yields at their station. U.S. citizens? No Doña Catarina immediately replies, as she nonchalantly hands him both hers and Refugia's green cards. He inspects the documents and the photos on the cards. With the cards still in his hands. He asks Doña Catarina, "Where are you going?" Puerto Isabel, Doña Catarina replies. She had been living in Port Isabel, for almost twenty years and understood English good enough to know what she was being asked by English speakers, though she herself spoke some of it. She really didn`t have much use for it. She lived in the Port Isabel neighborhood of Mexiquito, where the primary language spoken was Spanish. In fact, during those years no non-Spanish speakers lived in Mexiquito. She owned and operated a small grocery store. All her customers were Spanish speakers.

The next generation (her children and the other adult's friend's children) were bilingual Spanish and English speakers. They attended and were educated in the Port Isabel public schools where the speaking of Spanish was not allowed on school grounds. This generation had become fluent in both languages yet Spanish remained their dominant language.

What are you bringing back from Mexico? Medecinas (medicines), Doña Catarina, answered. Anything else? With their green cards still in his hand. No nada mas, she said. Doña Catarina was an imposing figure, who carried herself with lots of confidence and she dressed the part, too.

Whenever she went out in public to attend to personal affairs. She wore a nice dress, carried a stylish handbag, matching hat and gloves, as was the custom for women of means at the time. Consequently, she dressed Refugia, in the same style to fit the image of respectable ladies, for the purpose of the crossing.

Refugia kept her eyes looking straight ahead and sat very lady like with her hands on her lap. As she was coached to do by Doña Catarina. Seeing the lady like comport of the two passengers riding and being chauffeured by Mr. Cantu, who always wore a chauffeur type cap when driving his taxicab. The Immigration officer was satisfied that their documents were in order. He handed Dona Catarina back the green cards and waved them through.

Once they cleared the customs perimeter and were on Brownsville streets heading towards Port Isabel, Refugia, who had never been anywhere beyond the general vicinity of Linares, Mexico, began to shake uncontrollably. Doña Catarina, who was a commanding woman told Refugia, to get a hold of herself. She was safe now, that she did good and that they were soon going to be in Port Isabel, where she, her mother and sisters were going to start a new life.

She had to take her and leave her in Port Isabel, then return to Brownsville, with Mr. Cantu, to pick up her mother and sisters. Refugia regained her composure and thanked her aunt for all that she was doing for them.

Nighttime came for Pilar, her mother and Josefina. It was a moonless night. The inside of the dingy smelly hut was pitch dark. There were no lanterns, no candles, to light. They could not even see their hands in front of their faces. They continued with their whisper whimpering pleads and prayers to Christ and the Virgin Guadalupe. They dared not stir to leave the confines of the pitch-dark hut. They remained and stayed exactly where the coyote told them to stay. Not long after the final glow of the setting sun lost itself over the horizon and light gave way to darkness.

They began to hear low toned commanding voices and rushing footsteps rustling about outside on both sides of the hut. The voices faded; they heard water splashing. More thumping footsteps running back passed them.

Within moments, again, more low toned commanding voices, more rushing steps, more water splashing, more thumping, running feet back passed them.

The same rushing, splashing, running, thumping noises kept repeating themselves for what seemed like hours. But none of the directive voices were for them. None of the noises belonged to their coyote.

The fear of darkness, the fear of not knowing what all the strange noises all around them were. Alone and abandoned, they continued to pray for the return of their coyote. Hours they prayed. They prayed until fatigue and the sleep of night overcame them.

Suddenly, they were startled back awakened from their dozing state. The coyote had returned. He bursts into the hut stumbling and making hideous Ogre like grunting sounds. Pilar and her kin screamed in terror not knowing who the intruder was! The only thing they were able to visually distinguish in the pitch darkness was a bulky black figure standing at the entrance of the hut. His loud grumble identifying himself quiet's their frightened screams!

"Where were you?" Pilar asks him franticly, as they scramble to ready themselves to leave the hut and cross over to the United States.

The coyote had other plans. He reeked of liquor and stale smoke. Unable to speak clearly due to his stuporous state. The only sound he made were savage, animal like grizzly growls. He approaches them with arms and hands thrusting, gasping at the empty darkness in all directions to grab hold of one of the girls. Realizing they are in grave danger. They again began to scream and struggle blindly away from his reach.

He continues to aimlessly bumble in the darkness of the hut trying to take hold of one of them, in his crazed drunken nastiness. He had no preference. The only thing in his crazed mind was to violently gratify his reviling urge.

They kicked and punched at him. Somehow Pilar, in her frantic desperation to keep away from him as they scurried just out of his lunging reach. Her hands and fingers raking the dirt floor of the hut, hoping to find something, anything she could use as a weapon. She luckily finds something that feels like a stick. Taking hold of it with both hands, she begins to swing it as hard and as fast as she can.

With her adrenaline taking over. She stands and flails the stick as fast and hard as she can. She lands a solid blow. Not knowing what part of his body, she hits. She continues bashing away in rage, until she hears a moaning thump hit the ground in front of her. She continues whacking at the fallen coyote until she feels he is incapacitated. After a few more blows, she composes herself enough to call her mother and sister over to her.

They ran out of the hut.

With the stick still in one hand, her mother's hand in the other, and the sister clinging to the mother's other hand they run as fast as they can! A few strides later they find themselves on the riverbank. They stop. They dare not enter the water. Neither of them knew how to swim. They turn back to look in the direction of the craziness they had just escaped from. They hear the coyote groan as he flounders in pain, still inside the hut.

Pilar knows they don't have much time. The coyote will surely get back on his feet and come looking for them.

With racing pants and her heart now throbbing at her throat. She turns and looks upriver. All she sees is a curtain of blackness. She turns to look down river. She sees flickering lights off in the distance.

Without hesitation she yanks her mother's arm and begins a sprint along the riverbank for those yonder lights. Out of breath and their lungs feeling like they are about to burst. They stop to catch their breath. They stood at the edge of the riverbank catching their breath and wondering what to do next.

They see a group of people just ahead of them running out of the brush towards the river. They begin to enter the river one by one single file.

Pilar pulls her mother and sister to where the group is going into the river. When they get there, they see and hear another coyote yelling instructions at the water's edge. By the time they got there, about half of the migrants were chest high in the water walking towards the United States.

It was obvious that the coyote was familiar with shallow crossings. Hearing his commands, they run to get inline cutting in front of some who were in line to cross over. The coyote was looking at the migrants in the river and didn't notice Pilar, her mother and sister. Pilar tells them to keep their heads down and to not make eye contact with the coyote.

They pass right in front of him in the darkness. Lucky for them, the coyote was not concerned with looking for faces. He didn't know what any of his chickens looked like, nor did he care. He had already been paid. All he was interested in was to deliver the chickens to the river, point them to the U.S. side, get them in the water and get out of there as quickly as possible before the patrols came. Once the chickens get across.

Whatever happens after that is none of his concern. His job was done. Frankly, he could care less. As soon as the last one of the migrants is on the northern side of the river, he`s out of there. He does not wait around to see what happens after that.

Pilar, mother and sister follow the line of other migrants into the river. They feel the pull of the river`s strong undercurrent tugging at their legs and feet as it tries to tumble and carry them away. Pilar tells them to hold on tight. They move slowly, one step in front of the other. The group had linked hands forming a human chain. Some of the men in the group yelled words of encouragement to the rest. Repeatedly instructing them to keep moving, to not let loose of their grip.

One by one, they made it across. Pilar, mother and sister did not hear or see their demonic coyote anymore after that.

After finally making it across, soaked and covered from head to toe with the Rio Grande River`s brown water, and chocolate mud sediment. They clean themselves as best as they could. During the process of cleaning drying themselves. Pilar notices that the group is quickly splitting up.

People began running up the riverbank in all directions. Pilar asks several ladies in the group for directions towards Brownsville, but at that point and time it was "everyone for themselves". The sooner they got as far away from the river as they could, the better their chances of not being apprehended by Border Patrol, detained and sent back to Mexico. Pilar is bewildered not knowing where they were. Desperately, she kept asking people to point them towards Brownsville. No one listens. She has no other choice but to chase after some people as they ran up the river levee. when they reached the top of the levee. They catch up with two women who were walking as fast as they could to get far away from the river. One of the women appeared in her early teens and was just confused as Pilar. The other woman was older in her mid-twenties. She knew where she was going. It was apparent she had made the crossing before. The frightened young girl was totally dependent on her clinging as close to her as she could.

Pilar decided she was going to follow two women who were walking quickly away from them. every few moments the older women would turn back to look at Pilar and her kin following her. After a short distance. The older woman, yelled back over her shoulder and shouted at them to stop following. Pilar, shouted back in Spanish. Brownsville, Brownsville, where is Brownsville? Realizing that Pilar and her followers were not going to stop following. The older women lifted one of her arms and made a quick hand flash gesture and pointed towards a direction. Seeing this, Pilar, stopped to look to where the woman pointed. By the time Pilar, looked away from the direction to where the woman had pointed and back again to them. They had already scaled down the side of the levee out of sight. Pilar, mother and sister now found themselves all alone on top of the levee. Just like that. Within minutes of crossing the river. The entire group of people they crossed with had disappeared into the night. They stood there looking for the women. They were nowhere in sight. They had disappeared into the night and were journeying towards their destination.

They looked towards where the woman had pointed. They saw a domed glow over the horizon a distance off. They decided that it had to be Brownsville. They stayed on the levee continuing to walk towards the yellow hue.

Dawn came, followed by sunrise, followed by morning. They continued walking. They were close to Brownsville. They could see houses, they heard roosters crowing, dogs barking and motor vehicles rumbling.

Exhausted, thirsty and hungry they pressed on. They needed to get to Brownsville. Doña Catarina had told them she was going to come and get them. She had told them to find the corner of twelve Street and Elizabeth, in downtown Brownsville. She would be waiting there for them. Although Doña Catarina was fully aware of the coyote's unscrupulous nature but he was recommended to her. So, she went with the recommendation and made the deal with him. As is the case often when dealing with coyotes. It was a deal that had gone bad. Luckily, Pilar, mother and sister had survived the ordeal.

They see a vehicle speeding towards them. Not knowing who it was nor what to do. They quickly leave the levee road and run down the side of it. By the time they had reached the bottom of the bottom on the north side of it. The car was directly on the spot where they had climbed down. A man in uniform exited the car and began yelling at them in Spanish to stop.

He identified himself as Border Patrol. They obeyed the command and stood still. Scared and not knowing what was going to happen to them.

They sheepishly stood in place, huddled together. They had been captured. Josefina, and mother began to cry. They asked Pilar if they were going to jail. Or was the Border Patrol man going to send them back across the river? Pilar told them to remain calm. She didn't know what was coming next either?

The agent approached. He found three women, covered in dry river mud-clay and soot from head to toe. He had seen this picture many times before. Almost every time, he would either send back across the river on the spot or put them in his vehicle, drive them to the international bridge and make them walk back across into Mexico.

But this time for some unknown reason, the agent decided he would inquire and ask more questions of them. He asked them where they were from and why were they coming to the United States? Pilar did all the talking. Her mother was too scared, nervous and tongue tied. Her culture in Mexico, did not accustom her to speak often with other men besides her husband, or other male members of the immediate family, or the parish priest. Pilar told the Border Patrol agent that her father had been killed back in Linares. They had lost everything, and that they were coming over to live with an aunt. The agent asked Pilar where her aunt lived. Pilar said Puerto Isabel, he asked if she knew where Puerto Isabel was. Pilar said no, she did not know where Puerto Isabel was. He asked her if she didn't know where Puerto Isabel was, how were they going to get there? Pilar said her aunt had paid a coyote to cross them and bring them to the corner calles Elizabeth y doce.

She went on to tell the agent all about what the coyote had done to them and what he wanted to do to them, and what they did to get away from him. The agent asks Pilar, if the coyote did not cross them, how did they get across? The river is very dangerous, and you need to know where to cross. Pilar told the agent how they ran and ran after getting away from the coyote and not knowing where they were running from nor where they were running too. Said that after running for a long distance. They came across a group of migrants as they were being crossed by another coyote and they joined the group and crossed. He asked Pilar if they knew where they were now. Pilar said no. She hoped they were close to Brownsville. He asked if they had any idea of how to get to calles Elizabeth y doce (corner of twelve and Elizabeth streets)? Pilar said no. She told the agent she had a telephone number for her aunt and would call her if she could find a telephone. But she said her aunt was not at home she was waiting for them at Elizabeth y doce.

The agent told Pilar, how they were in a lot of trouble and how her aunt was in a lot of trouble as well for crossing them into the United States, illegally. At that point the tears just started to flow from Pilar's eyes and down her face. Streaks of mud ran down both of cheeks. Seeing the cascading tears from Pilar, and how mother and sister were also overcome with emotion, their faces hair and dresses a muddy mess.

For some reason something that sometimes happens to some men when they see a women cry. One woman crying in front of a man is bad enough. But the agent had three women sobbing uncontrollably, under his authority. He told them to stop crying. He still had some more questions for them, and he needed them to be able to answer?

Pilar said she was crying because she didn't want her aunt to get into any kind of trouble with the autoridades (authorities). She had taken extreme measures in bringing them to the United States. And she didn't want anything bad to happen to her? Pilar told the agent, that they would willingly return to Mexico. If it meant that her aunt would not be arrested. All her aunt wanted to do was help them, because they didn't have anyone else to turn to for assistance.

The agent looked at Josefina. He surmised that she was a pre-teen of about ten years of age or so. He asked Pilar how old she was. Pilar said she was fifteen years old. He did not ask for Josefina's age. There was no need to.

He ordered them to get in the back seat of his car. They did as were ordered. They sat in silence. Josefina asked Pilar where the official was taking them. Pilar said she didn't know. Pilar suspected that he was going to take them to jail. She had no inclination that border patrol agents often took their detainees to the international bridge and released them to walk back into Mexico.

She asked the agent, "Are you taking us to the "carcel" (jail)? No the agent replied. I am driving you to the bridge and releasing you there. You are retuning back to Mexico." Pilar was somewhat relieved. At least they weren't going to jail. At this point, after all the horror and hardship they had just experienced, Matamoros was a welcome relief. Even if they didn't know anyone there. She felt that once back in Mexico, they would maybe be able to figure some way to survive. Any place in Mexico, was better than jail in the U.S.

Pilar then began to think about her aunt and all the terrible trouble she was in now in because of them. She politely asked the agent that if they were being returned to Mexico, did that mean that her aunt would no longer be in trouble with the "authoridades?" The agent replied that once he took them to the bridge and they walked back to Mexico, he had no way of knowing who their aunt was. So, if he didn't know who her aunt was, he couldn't arrest her? Pilar, again in her polite tone of voice, said "gracias senor". She also told him how sorry they were for causing him any trouble. The Border Patrol agent did not say anything back to Pilar, he just kept driving.

Within a matter of minutes Pilar, mother and sister, realize that they are right smack in the middle of a city. They had never been to any city other than Linares. Linares was an old Mexican town with old Mexican town features. However, Brownsville too is a city that had been established and populated many years ago. It was a modern town by their standards. The streets were all paved, rows and rows of houses lined each side of the street they were driving on. They noticed that the houses were not built of adobe. Some were made of brick and others were made of wood. And they were all painted, mostly, white with different colors for the trim.

The agent turns off the street he was driving on and goes into an alley. He stops his car between two tall buildings. Still sitting behind the wheel. He turns his body sides ways to face them. "When you get out of the car, walk straight ahead until you get to the street. That will be twelve street. When you get to the street, walk left to the end of the block. That will be the corner of twelve and Elizabeth. But before you get out. You must promise me one thing". "Si senor," Pilar answered.

"You have to promise me that when you get to Puerto Isabel, you will enroll in school." "Si, si, I promise. We will enroll in school. Muchas gracias senor, que Dios me lo bendiga." (Thank you sir, God Bless you). Yeah, yeah, gracias, the agent said back. I will wait here until you get to twelve Street and walk left. Now Go! Get out of my car!

As soon as he gave them the go command, Pilar flung the back door open and pulled mother and sister out of the car behind her. They walked with a quickened haste, reached the street and turned left. As soon as they got to the corner of twelve and Elizabeth, they stood there looking up and down both streets hoping to see their aunt. As Pilar stood there looking in all four directions for Doña Catarina, she saw the Border Patrol agent's car come to the intersection of twelve and the alley. The car went right and sped away in the opposite direction. That was the last time they saw the agent. As he sped away. Pilar, made the sign of the cross on herself, said a silent prayer for him and thanked God Jesus and the Virgin Guadalupe, for sending an Angel, to their rescue.

The sun was midway between the morning horizon and noon. People were beginning to crowd the downtown streets on their way to work and shopping. Cars were filling up the parking spaces, smelly gasoline emissions began to trap between the canyon of downtown buildings, the echoing blare of car horns bouncing off the busy business district walls captivated and amazed Pilar, her mother and her sister, as they stood with their backs pressed against one of the buildings` like frighten, disoriented kittens, as they did their best to stay clear of the sidewalk path being used by the downtown pedestrians.

People walked briskly passed them in both directions, without paying any attention to them. Seeing migrants who had just crossed over was a common sight in downtown Brownsville. They were pretty much left alone, as long as they did not impede the pedestrian flow, or panhandle, or crowd and block the entry way to businesses. Shoppers knew and had become accustomed to the fact that by the time they came back out of the store they would be gone. Although it was not unusual to see recent migrants' downtown, the numbers were not many. For the most part migrants from Mexico, pretty much stayed on the fringes of the city after crossing over. Those who did venture through downtown stayed in the shadows of the building`s side streets and alleys.

Out of nowhere a taxi car makes a sudden stop right off the sidewalk curb where Pilar, her mother and sister were standing against the wall. Doña Catarina was sitting on the front passenger seat. "Vengan muchachas, rapido, suvanse" (hurry girls get in)! Tia! Pilar yelled in relived excitement. Again, Pilar quickly dashes to back door of the taxi, with mother and sister in tow, she opens it, shoves Josefina in followed by her mother before jumping in herself.

No sooner had she slammed the car door closed behind her than the driver, Mr. Cantu, pushed his foot down on the gas pedal zooming off darting, passing, from between cars like a bank robber driving a getaway car.

In no time at all the taxi car was out of Brownsville city limits streaking on the twenty-five-mile-long highway towards Port Isabel.

Mr. Cantu was a stogie chomping, medium sized inky potbellied adventurous gambler, who happened to be a better driver than he was a gambler. He was an especially, popular car for hire, into Mexico, with the shrimpers and fisherman after payday. They trusted him to drive them to Matamoros, take them to all the good time places and back again. He had a good reputation of being able to outmaneuver and evade the

Mexican police. There were many stories of how Mr. Cantu had driven his drunk rowdy shrimper passengers safely back across after a bottle smashing, furniture busting bar brawl.

With all four car windows rolled down on the accelerated taxi. The salty Gulf of Mexico, wind rushed in, creating a churning, swoosh inside the car making it difficult to hear any exchange of words inside the car. But Doña Catarina did not think for a moment to ask Mr. Cantu, to roll up the windows to the car so that she and her relatives, could have a conversation. She knew Mr. Cantu, they were old acquaintances, going back many years. She knew that the last thing Mr. Cantu wanted to hear was the storied words of her sister-in-law and nieces no matter how adventurous.

He was a taxicab driver and like most taxicab drivers, all they wantedto do is get their fare from point A to point B. They are not at all interested in the personal affairs of their passengers. So, Doña Catarina, sat patiently in the front passenger seat, as the briny wind twirled and agitated hers and her sister-in-law's salt and pepper speckled hair, along with the long cascading raven indigenous Mare of her nieces.

Thirty minutes later they were in Port Isabel. Mr. Cantu made his way to Mexiquito, zig zagging his car over and around the many oyster shell filled pot holes of the powdery, salty, dirt, streets of the barrio. After a short bouncy ride, the car finally comes to a jerking halt, in front of "La Copa de Oro", Doña Catarina's grocery store.

Without turning around to look at her relatives. Doña Catarina announces that they have reached their destination and to disembark the car. She reaches inside of her handbag and pulls out a roll of paper money. She uncoils the bills, counts out some of them, hands them over to Mr. Cantu, who takes the bills and stuffs them in his shirt pocket. She thanks him for his service and exits the car. He says, "De nada", pushes his foot down on the gas paddle, leaving behind a dark gray smelly chocking plume that Doña Catarina, and her relatives briskly fan away from faces.

Pilar, mother and sister stand sheepishly bunched together on the dirt street in front of the store. They wait for Doña Catarina's next directive. She points to an entry door on a building that is connected to the "Copa de Oro." The connecting building is Doña Catarina's, house. She had added the store part years later. Inside of both buildings ran a connecting hallway Doña Catarina, used to get from her living quarters to the store and back to her house.

She pointed to the front door of the house, that was open with a screen door as it's anterior entry and made a waving hand gesture for them to move towards it. They turned and made haste with Doña Catarina, behind. She called ahead to them to go straight in, the door was not lashed. During those days no one in Mexiquito, lashed or locked their screen doors, there was no need for it. Breaking and entry into someone's home for the sake of stealing, was unheard of.

They walk in and gaze at Doña Catarina, who was the last one to enter, turned to close screen door behind her. She looked back across the dusty street to her neighbors' houses. As was expected and the norm for Mexiquito, residents, curious neighbors, were all looking through parted front living room flowery curtains, and from behind the obscured protection of their screen doors. Some neighbor ladies, the more inquisitive ones had even come outside to sprinkle rainwater they kept stored in buckets and barrels on their much cherished, cared for medicinal herbs. Others came out to sweep the front porch and walkway path to the front gate. This way they could get a better look at or hear any conversation Doña Catarina, and her newly arrived relatives were having.

Any information they could get on the new visitors, would be needed as psychological conversation, gossip, stress release, during the ritualistic afternoon merienda, (sweetbread and coffee. Like afternoon biscuits and tea). It was customary with Mexiquito, women, to have their after siesta, mid-afternoon coffee and fresh hot sweetbread from the local bakery to perk away the drowsiness. Of course, they also always needed new gossip to share as they sipped coffee and ate sweet tasting pastries. They would talk about the number of relatives Doña Catarina brought to her house, who transported them? How did they look? Were they frail? Big, small, tall, short, skinny, fat, light skinned, dark skinned, young, old, middle age? Also add any other pertinent information.

The first order of business for Pilar, after settling in to live with Doña Catarina, was to enroll her sisters in school, make sure her mother was comfortable, and then find a job. Her aunt being the wise woman that she was knew that four women living on their own in Linares, Mexico, was not a good situation. They had no one to protect them, they had no one to provide for them, so she told them they could not remain there. She told them they were coming to the United States to live with her.

The next day Pilar went with Doña Catarina, to enroll Refugia, and Josefina in school. Pilar did not enroll. Even if she wanted to, which she did. She knew that she couldn't. Her aunt had already been very kind, generous and shown great courage and responsibility for their safety and welfare. It was now up to her to find a job in order to provide financially for her mother and sisters. She was a big girl of fifteen and very capable of finding work.

The day after enrolling her sisters in school. She found and went to work as a cook's helper in a restaurant. During her days off, she headed shrimp in the local fish houses during the shrimping season. When she was laid off from work at the restaurant. She cleaned houses, worked as a nanny and many other jobs. Doña Catarina provided a home for them to live in and for this Pilar, remained forever grateful.

It did not take long for Pilar and her family to become welcome members of the Mexiquito community. They were part of Doña Catarina's family now. That meant that they were all to receive the same respect and courtesies as Doña Catarina and her children. They made friends with the other girls in the neighborhood.

Pilar's first encounter with Merced Cantu Jr., who years later became her husband, happened when she was eighteen years old. She was running an errand for her aunt Doña Catarina whose eldest, Genaro, worked on the opposite side of town where the Anglo population lived and had businesses. It was the middle of the day; her errand was to bring Genaro his lunch. Merced Jr. was driving a fare in one of his father's taxis. He happened to see the beautiful Pilar walking under the hot noon sun. He knew who Pilar was, she had lived in Port Isabel for three years now.

Everyone in Mexiquito, as well as the whole of Port Isabel, for that matter knew each other except that the Anglos lived in their part of town where most of the Mexican Americans lived in their Mexiquito side of town.

Merced had admired Pilar from afar, but he had not yet had an opportunity to get close to her. Pilar also knew who Merced Jr was but she didn't have an interest in him nor any other young man at the time. She was totally focused on her jobs and providing for her sisters. A year after coming to Port Isabel, their mother died of cancer. The loss of her mother, when she was sixteen, made her more driven to work and provide for her sisters.

Merced was aware that Pilar was the older sister who took care of her younger sisters. He also knew that she and her sisters lived with Doña Catarina, a lady highly respected who was protective of the girls. Pilar blossomed into a beautiful senorita who had attracted Merced's interest.

The more he saw and thought of her, the more interested he became. He began to drive past her house when he went on a call to drive a fare somewhere hoping to get a glimpse of her.

He had not yet summoned the courage to approach Doña Catarina to ask her permission to call on Pilar. Doña Catarina was a woman of strong moral character with a no-nonsense attitude. Merced knew he would be in for a serious sit-down question-and-answer drilling as to his intentions for Pilar.

He had heard the story about the time when Pilar was working picking cotton on one of the cotton fields outside of Los Fresnos, TX. The Border Patrol was on one of their regular roundups in search of illegals. They drove to the field with their paddy wagons. The labor contractor who had taken Pilar and other people from Port Isabel to the field was somehow able to get word back to Port Isabel, that the "migra" (Border Patrol) was at the field detaining illegals. As soon as Doña Catarina heard about the roundup, she called Mr. Cantu and his taxi. They immediately zoomed over to the field. Luckily for Pilar, a woman and man called her over to them as they are waiting their turn to be questioned as to their legal citizenship status. When Mr. Cantu and Doña Catarina arrived at the work site, she found Pilar and the couple. She grabbed Pilar and began to walk away with her. A Border Patrol agent sees Doña Catarina and Pilar walking away towards the taxi where Mr. Cantu waited with the motor running and ready to drive off as soon as Doña Catarina got in the car. The agent called out to them to stop. Doña Catarina, with Pilar in tow, continued walking. The agent caught up to them. Angered because Doña Catarina dared to walk away, he demanded to see their papers. Doña Catarina ordered Pilar to get in the taxi. She then turned to talk to the agent. She showed him her legal papers. When the agent asks for Pilar`s papers, she told him that Pilar was her niece, a minor, was under her custodianship. When the agent asks if Pilar was a U.S. Citizen, Doña Catarina affirmed that she was. When he asked where they`re from, she replied that they were from Port Isabel. She turned her back on the agent once again, then proceeded to get into the taxi.

Pilar had been sitting on the back passenger side looking out the car window and listening to her aunt and the agent exchange words. She was afraid, not knowing what to expect, not knowing what was going to happen to her and her aunt.

After a few more words back and forth between her aunt and the agent, she turned her back on him, opened the door, told Pilar to slide over, got in and ordered Mr. Cantu to drive off. He floors it. The back tires spun on the loose sandy soil before the rear tires grip the surface and they sped off.

The agent was left standing in a whirlwind of cotton field dust waving his hands in the air yelling at Doña Catarina. Pilar turned back to look at the agent as Mr. Cantu piloted his getaway car off the cotton field and onto the black top farm-to-market road. Pilar turned around and saw him remove his western hat and slap the dirt off his off his neatly pressed green uniform.

Merced decided that he would take his chances on an opportunity to meet her somewhere as she went to and from her daily tasks. After all, Port Isabel was a small town and Mexiquito, even smaller.

Everyone in Mexiquito attended the same socials and wedding receptions. The problem, however, is that all the young girls who attended socials were always chaperoned by mothers, Godmothers, grandmothers and aunts.

Merced`s patience finally paid off one hot steamy, sunny day. Pilar was bringing her cousin his lunch. The scrooching noon sun became his friend that day. On his way to drop off his rider, he happened to pass Pilar as she was leaving Mexiquito. Merced seized the moment. He quickly dropped off his fare and sped back to catch up to Pilar.

He approached slowly from the rear until he came up alongside her. Pilar ignored him at first when he asks her where she was going. She ignored him because it was none of his business. She was on an errand and thought it was rude of him to inquire. She kept walking. He asked if she wanted a ride to where she was going but Pilar kept walking, without answering.

Keeping pace with his taxi next to her, he convinced her the taxi was much easier than walking in the hot sun.

When she accepted a ride to Bob's Garage, he drove slower than usual. He wanted to make the ride last with her as long as possible. He kept peeking back at her with his rear-view mirror. Pilar started to feel uneasy. She had never been alone in a car with a man before, so she turned her face and looked out the window instead hoping they would get to Bob`s Garage soon.

Merced tried to start up a conversation by making small talk, about the dog days, the annoying sandstorms that frequently forced Port Isabel, residents to shut themselves in their homes, and other happenings. Pilar's reply answers were all one-word answers.

When they arrived at Bob's, Pilar took the lunch to her cousin. Once back in the taxi, Merced asked, "Who was the lunch for?"

"My cousin." Now we're getting somewhere Merced, thinks to himself. She answered with two words instead of one.

Merced talked all the way on the drive back. Pilar, sensing he was trying a bit too hard to impress her shut down. She didn't have time for a suitor just yet.

Time passed. Pilar was busy with her jobs. She began to study the school textbooks her sister brought home from school. With some tutoring from them, she learned to read and write English. She valued the importance of an education and made sure her sisters went to school. She herself had studied up to the first year of secundaria in Mexico, middle school in the U.S. so her reading, writing and math skills were good. She started a study group in the neighborhood with other girls in the same situation. She would borrow some of her sister's textbooks and bring them with her to the study sessions.

When Pilar turned eighteen, Doña Catarina sent her and Refugia back to Mexico to start their immigration legalization process. Their younger sister Josefa was unable to go with them. She began to have epileptic seizures in school. Back then school officials in Port Isabel didn't know how to deal with epileptic students. She was sent to a state school in Abilene, where she stayed until she was eighteen. A few months later Pilar and Refugia were back in Matamoros with their legal documents.

Merced continued to pursue his interest in Pilar, but nothing really serious developed. Pilar was not ready for courtship. Around this same time, the Korean War broke out. Shortly afterwards the U.S. military draft board rounded up all the able-bodied young men eighteen years and up. Merced was in that group. They were taken for their physical, and those who were deemed physically fit for military service were shipped off to boot camp.

They didn't see each other again until after the war ended three years later. A big welcome home military parade was held in their honor. The entire town turned out to welcome and cheer their heroes back home.

There were red, white and blue banners hanging from every lamp post, starting at the entrance of town and all the way to the end of Main Street.

She was amazed at the patriotism displayed by the townspeople. Never before had she seen anything like it. She saw Merced among the marching formation of returning veterans. He looked different. There was a proud swagger in his step and rank stripes on the arms of his starched pressed uniform. The smile, however, was the same wide toothy one she remembered from the last time they saw each other three years ago. She noticed he was sporting a neatly trimmed Pedro Infante mustache (popular Mexican singer/actor during the golden age of Mexican cinema in the 1940s).

Up until that part of the march, Merced was more caught up in the pomp and circumstance of the moment than anything else. But when she waved at him, it fanned the memories of before the war.

After the parade the entire town was invited for refreshments and hot dogs in a section of downtown where a street was closed to traffic. A street dance followed, and the celebration continued into the night. Pilar and Merced found each other, shared hot dogs and pop, found two empty chairs and sat down to drink eat and talk. A lot had happened in the three years he was gone, there was much news to catch up with. The music played, people danced, laughed and had a good time. Pilar and Merced did not dance. All they wanted to do was talk. When it was time for Pilar to return home, she agreed that Merced walk her home.

A few days after the welcome homecoming parade, Merced was back helping his father by driving a taxi. The war had changed him. He had seen, gone through and survived the horrors of battle after battle in Korea. He had left Port Isabel as an idealistic teenager, thinking war was some gun-toting adventure, firing bullets at the enemy, like he saw in romanticized Hollywood war movies.

Instead, he came back a man, who had to deal with all the mental and physical scars war veterans bring home with them and have to live with the rest of their lives.

He needed a sense of normalcy. He needed to get his life back in order. He was twenty-one years of age. A man with aspirations. He could no longer go back home to live under his father's roof. He didn't belong there anymore.

He asked Doña Catarina for her permission to call on Pilar. She gave her approval but told him the matter was up to Pilar. She had no intention of assuming the role as matchmaker. Any communications and intentions he had for Pilar needed to be between him and Pilar.

The courtship lasted two years. Pilar was in love with Merced and wanted to marry him, but she needed to wait for her sisters to become old enough to work, marry or both. She did not want them to be a financial burden on their aunt. Merced agreed. He loved Pilar. He would wait for her as long as it took.

The time for matrimony arrived. He had saved enough for her dress and a small wedding reception. It was going to be a civil ceremony. A Catholic wedding required them to go and sit with the local priest, who would go through the whole interrogation and lecture process of marriage.

He asked his aunt to go to Brownsville and buy the prettiest dress she could find with the money he gave her. Instead of the traditional white dress, for some inexplicable reason, she came back with a pink one. She took it to Pilar and told her that was her wedding dress. As soon as Pilar saw the pink dress, she knew something was wrong. She knew all first-time brides in Mexico, as well as in the United States, get married in a white dress. After a lot of pleading from Merced, Pilar married in her pink wedding dress.

After several years as a homemaker and mother, she decided she wanted to help with the family income. She went to work for Bayside Net and Twine. She was put on a line along with other women, spinning twine that would later be used by the net makers. One time she lost the tip of one of fingers caught in the twine.

Pilar worked for seventeen years. Her spinning contributed towards the making of thousands of shrimping nets. She's proud of the many years she worked in the net making industry. She then went to work for the school district as a cook.

"We made sure the meals we served the children were nutritious and delicious because the children we were feeding were our own as well as the children of our friends and neighbors. When it comes to food children are the best critics. They will tell you right away when something doesn't taste good and they are not going to eat it. They will leave it on the plate and throw it away."

After retiring from the school kitchen, Pilar became a stay-at-home wife again. By that time her children had grown, finished their education and married.

Merced had built a thriving auto mechanic business with their sons as partners. The daughters married good hard-working men. She was happy staying at home. She had worked for more than half of her life.

Her sisters were well with families of their own. They remained close knit. She made sure of that. They celebrated holidays and birthdays together as a family. After Sunday Mass, all her children and her children's children come home.

Merced is gone now. Pilar has a son, Rafael, who lives with her. She is happy and grateful for the many years she and Merced shared as loving husband and wife. She is proud of her children, grandchildren and great-grandchildren. She is thankful to the United States for the opportunities they had to succeed and have a good life. She takes pride in Merced's military service as well as her son-in-law and grandson who are now serving their country.

11

Marcella Casanova

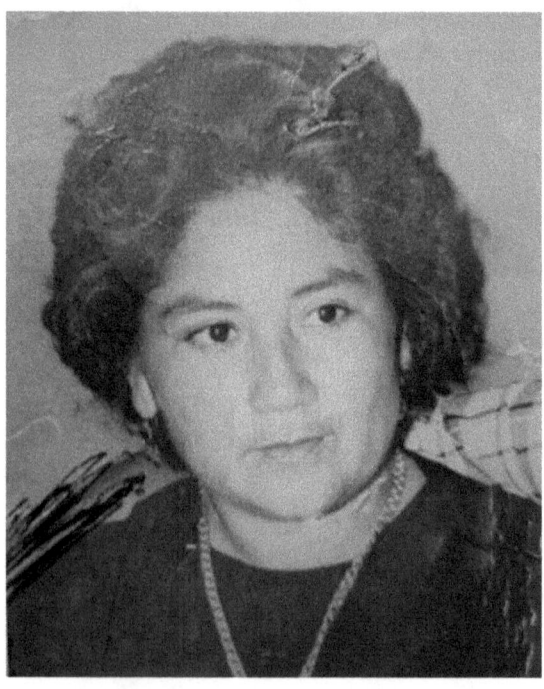

On 10 January 1973, Carlos "Boy" Casanova fell overboard. He was fishing on the *Inshala*. The tragedy happened while he was bringing in the rigging to head home. He couldn't swim and he was lost at sea.

On 01 June 2021, three of his five brothers spoke of the love of their mother, the pain she bore and the void that Boy's loss created in the family.

The painful memory of that tragic day never completely goes away. "Life as we knew it completely changed us all. He was the oldest. We all looked up to him. His loss gravely impacted all who knew him." He was a local boy who grew up in Port Isabel, known and loved by many. The memories shared and the strong family ties are a testament to their mother's strength, love and resilience.

Marcella did not have an easy life but her faith, goodwill and strength of character lives on in her children and grandchildren.

"God loaned them to me," she told her son Leo when referring to Boy and another son Nikki who died young. Until the end of her life, she visited and tended her sons' grave sites every day. She prayed to God for strength. She had four other sons to live for. She never overtly expressed any bitterness towards her sons and her fate in life. She chose to cherish the time God gave her with her sons here on earth. Rather than being resentful and giving in to an emotionally depressed existence, Marcella adopted a jovial outlook on life. She became a matriarch mother to her remaining children, grandchildren and matron aunt to many nieces and nephews. Many of Marcella`s nieces and nephews had lost a parent when they were young children. She made it her mission to give them unconditional love. She understood that a parent`s love can never be replaced by anyone else. She had an uncanny manner in providing support by giving counsel and advice, telling her nieces and nephews stories about their deceased parent. Until her final day Marcella remained the beloved aunt who was always there for them.

The brothers said their mother never talked about their loss. She buried her pain deep in her heart and only she knew the piercing heartache of a mother who had lost a son at sea. He was never found. Every year on the anniversary of Boy`s drowning. Marcella would return to the shore of Padre Island and wait, and pray, and wait some more.

Marcella returned to Padre Island in 1999. This time, twenty-six years after Boy's loss, she found the "El Cristo de Los Pescadores (Christ of the Fisherman statue)." He had his arms stretched out wide and a plaque carried the prayer. "Father! Receive the souls of these brave fisherman who sailed through this pass and never returned."

For the first time since 1973, Marcella realized that she was not standing alone on the shore of Padre Island looking out to sea. Christ was there like he had been for all those many years she mourned her son Boy. The pleading words went straight to her heart. She felt his presence. She returned home that day fully realizing that Boy was truly at home with God. Three of the brothers said they heard what happened, although in our interview with them, they found out, they had all heard different versions. "Our cousin Mingo told me what happened," Jerry said. "He and Michael Boudreaux were also on the boat. Mr. Alegre was the captain. It was a Zimmerman boat. Mingo told me that Boy was the rig man and fell into shark-infested waters. It was cold."

"No," Nacho interjected. "They were coming home, about twenty miles north of the jetties at the time. He was taking in the rigging. It was rough, cold and windy. A wave caught the net and jerked him into the sea. He couldn't swim and had always been afraid of the water."

"So, when Boy went down, there was no other boat near them?" Jerry asked.

"No, they were coming in. When he fell overboard, I had just come in from shrimping. The Gulf was rough," Nacho remembered.

"We were both in the military when it happened," Leo added. "I was in California and Jerry was at Kelly Air Force Base in San Antonio."

"One of our mother's first concerns was for Nacho. He ran up and down the beach yelling for Boy... he was hoping that since Boy had fallen overboard while they were coming in that maybe he had gotten hold of something that floated, a log or something. Nacho yelled for Boy for hours," Jerry added. "Nacho then borrowed a boat from someone and went back out and continued searching for him."

A year before their youngest brother, Nikki, had died at school. He was only fifteen years old; he had a heart condition. Jerry was in Germany at the time. Leo was home on leave, and they were at a baseball game. "We were sitting high in the bleachers. He fell backwards. When I got to him, he was already passing away."

Boy had married Maurilia and they had two daughters, Veronica and Vanessa when he died.

"There were only two times when our mom expressed her feelings. One was her antipathy toward our dad and the other was her fear of losing the connection with Boy's daughters. They were the first grandchildren, and she couldn't face the thought of not having them in her life. But Maurilia, thank God, had no intention of taking her children away from their dad's family."

The brothers agreed that their mother never spoke directly of her loss.

Marcella had met their father, Carlos Casanova, on a Padre Island beach. He was a bay fisherman who had come to Port Isabel, from Veracruz, Mexico. After they married, they moved to Veracruz. The older sons were born there. When the family moved back to Port Isabel, their father Carlos didn't come with them.

Jerry, Nacho and Leo all agreed that he never provided any financial support for them. In the beginning, he was barely making money fishing, but even after he began making money, he never sent any home.

Marcella gave birth to six sons – Boy (Carlos Jr.), Jerry, Nacho, Leo, Javier and Nikki - and after Carlos Sr. abandoned her, she raised the family on her own. With no support from him, they lived in poverty.

Carlos spent most of his time in the southern Gulf of Mexico and eventually bought a home there and started another family.

The sons agreed that their dad was unlike most shrimpers. While most would rather be home with family, he loved shrimping so much that he just wanted to be out at sea. Their mother was left at home to cope with both the responsibility of raising six sons and the financial burden.

"We used to bounce around from family to family. We had no home so we lived with whoever would have us. We ended up in Bayside. Dad finally bought a piece of land there and we built a house, more like a shack but it was our home. No more living in other family's houses" Jerry explained. "We had a little wagon. Boy and I would go get water. We had no running water at home. Mom would have to bathe us outside in a tub, one at a time."

"She never showed any kind of hardship, nor did she ever complain. We never knew how she ate or if she ate but she always made sure that we had food," Jerry said. She worked many years as a housekeeping maid at *White Sands Motel*."

"But she was tough. We were afraid to disobey her," Nacho added.

They willingly took turns with whatever chores she assigned to them. They had a Volkswagen Beetle and when it would break down, mom knew a mechanic who would fix it and when she couldn't pay, he would come to their home and demand payment. The boys all remembered those incidents, the many hard times. But they never let any of their friends see them as poor kids in need of pity or handouts. Their mother made sure of that. She had a stubborn pride about her. She made them all tough and taught them survival skills.

"I remember I would have to fix six sandwiches for school in the mornings," Nacho said.

We always had food to eat even if she had to ask Mr. Raymond, the grocer, for six slices of bologna. He would allow her to take groceries on credit. When Carlos Sr. came, he would pay the bill.

They all agreed that none of their friends had any money either back then, so they never really noticed how poor they were. They were all in the same boat as far as poverty was concerned.

"We always wanted to make Mom happy. I remember when I was in Junior High, one of the administrators came into our science class and asked for a volunteer to help in the cafeteria. In return, we'd get out of the science class with an A and receive two free meal passes for the year. I was the first to raise my hand. I knew Mom would be proud of me for providing lunches for Nacho and me for the year," Jerry said.

"She always made sure we had food for lunch. If she didn't have anything to make sandwiches, she'd cook something and bring it to school. I was always happy to see her coming to the school at lunch time," Leo remembered. "Because I was sure she was bringing something tasty for us to eat. She was a great cook."

She loved Tarpon football. She never missed a game at home or away. Even after we moved to Los Fresnos, she continued going to Tarpon games. She was related to half the town. She knew that she could visit with family and friends and find out how everyone was doing.

Everything she did, she did for the boys, and they recognized her commitment.

"She never beat around the bush," they all agreed. "She always said exactly what was on her mind and she meant every word. She was proud of all of us. She made sure we never missed a day of school. We all got awards for perfect attendance every year." Leo's comment brought laughter from all three.

When they grew up, three of the sons joined the service. Jerry went into the Air Force while Leo and Javier served in the Navy. Nacho immediately chose shrimping as his career after high school.

Nacho, who spent his life as a captain. spoke of her constant fear for him. "She wanted me to quit shrimping."

Although their dad failed to provide any support for the boys, they maintained a relationship with him. He was demanding and, therefore, difficult to work with. They did appreciate that he taught them how to shrimp.

They agreed that he was a good man but totally focused on work. All but the younger ones ended up working with him. It would always be just Carlos Sr. and one son on the boat. Working a Gulf shrimp boat with a two-man crew was not an uncommon thing back in the '50s, '60s and '70s. It was not recommended for obvious safety reasons, but it happened a lot.

Today boat owners will not let their boats leave the dock unless they have a three-man crew minimum. The risk is too high. Two-man crews are asking for trouble. If an accident happens on a boat being worked by a two-man crew, the owner would most likely be looking at a lawsuit.

The owner will lose because he or she should have never allowed the boat to leave the dock with only two men on board.

"I remember one time Dad was working for Sammy Snodgrass. We were in Campeche when the boat started sinking," Jerry related. "My dad called the Coast Guard, and they came from New Orleans. In the meantime, we bailed out water with the buckets we had on board. When the Coast Guard arrived, they pumped the water out. We saved the boat.

Marcella Casanova met the love of her life on Padre Island beach. They married and had six sons. The man she loved may have loved her too. But as fate would have it; he loved the sea more. Ironically, her first born Carlos, Jr. also loved the sea.

She lost both to the sea. The husband sailed off as far as he could to a land far away and never returned. The son went into the depths of the same sea where his remains still lay today.

12

Maria Luisa Chavez

Maria Luisa and her husband Federico owned and operated a net-making and repair business out of their home. Before that she worked at *Bayside Net and Twine* for thirteen years. She was a net inspector. She inspected every net before it shipped to the buyer. The reputation for the high-quality nets of *Bayside Net and Twine* was in her hands and in her eyes.

If a flawed net got past her and sent to the buyer, the integrity of the net maker and its standing in the industry was at stake. More importantly, many jobs were on the line. *Bayside Net and Twine* had an excellent and proud reputation throughout the shrimping world, as being one of the best net making companies in the industry. They sold their nets to every shrimping port in the U.S. They also had a big market with the shrimpers in Mexico.

Whenever Luisa found a defect in one of the nets, she repaired it. She did not send it back to the net maker. It was unproductive to do so. That would cause a back-and-forth delay in productivity. She would, however, let the net maker know what she found and how she fixed it.

The snags in the nets were mostly small kinks, a crimp here and there. They were few, minor and far between. The net makers at Bayside Net and Twine were the best in the business. These men grew up with net webbing dangling from their hands and fingers.

They were skilled craftsmen who took great pride in their work. Any blemish, no matter how small, found with their nets was personal to them. They had been making fishing nets since before the shrimping industry began. They were experts at making all kinds of nets. They had grown up learning and apprenticing with their fathers, grandfathers and other local master net makers. They knew how to make gill nets, cast nets, coracle nets, hand nets, saline nets and now deep trawling nets. This made Luisa's job easier.

Luisa was good at repairing nets. She learned by helping her husband. He had a small net mending shop in the back yard of their home. Before that, he worked for Bill and Walter Zimmerman making and repairing nets for the Las Cruz's shrimping fleet. The Cruzes shrimping boats were recognized without a doubt as the best if not one of the best fleets in the industry. They were referred to as Las Cruz`s because every boat in their fleet has the word Cruz as part of their name. Cruz is the Spanish word for Cross (*Vera Cruz, Plata Cruz, Salina Cruz, Fiesta Cruz, Dorada Cruz*, etc.). Before that he worked for Mr. Wallace Boudreaux and *Valley Frozen Foods*, mending their nets.

After Louisa finished her eight-to-five job at *Bayside Net and Twine*, she went home. After supper, she joined her husband in the net shop. Usually, after supper, Federico would go back to the shop to mend some more, clean up the shop and prep for the next day. Luisa swept, picked up and stacked net remnants and helped tread the flat net needles with twine. They used that time to talk about their day and the kids.

Luisa enjoyed watching Federico work. She loved and admired him. He was a hard worker, a loving husband and ideal father. They came to the U.S. from Madero Tamaulipas, Mexico. She was twenty-three, Federico was twenty-five when they moved to Port Isabel. They brought with them a few belongings. The most valued and precious possession they brought was three-year-old Federico Chavez, Jr. They immediately began to seek employment. Like all immigrants who come in search of a better life, they brought little more than the clothes on their backs and a lot of determination.

After many years of hard work in shrimping-related jobs, they were able to save enough money to purchase a city lot. After that they continued to save. They contracted a home builder to construct a brick home that she still lives in today.

When Luisa and Federico immigrated from Mexico, neither of them spoke a word of English. In fact, till this day they still do not speak English. They understand some and can communicate, when necessary, but they do not converse in English. Everyone in town they dealt with spoke Spanish. As their sons got older and became fluent in both English and Spanish, they translated for them.

Luisa's first job was working in a shrimp processing plant. Federico hired on as a header on a shrimp boat. One shrimping trip into the Gulf of Mexico was all it took for Federico to realize shrimping was not for him.

After the completion of his one and only shrimping trip, he found a master net maker and mender by the name of Don Juan Gonzalez. Mr. Gonzalez needed someone to help him around the shop. He hired Federico as an apprentice. He cleaned up, treaded net needles, carried and delivered finished nets to the boats, and anything else he was told to do. In between his menial duties, the master net maker taught him some stiches. The pay wasn't much but at least he wasn't out on the Gulf of Mexico.

Federico and Luisa did everything together. They developed their close unbreakable bond because when they came from Mexico, it was just the two of them with their small child in a strange land. A young family on their own; little money, no friends, no place to live, no job. All they had was each other.

When Federico found his job on the shrimp boat, he left Luisa and little Federico behind. They lived in a small, one room rental in the Mexiquito section of town. All those days that Federico was gone shrimping were miserable days for Luisa. She had little Freddy for company and comfort. But without Federico being home, she felt as if the family was not complete. There was an empty void. She wanted her family to be whole and for Federico to be at home with them.

After that one trip, Federico and Luisa never spent another day or night apart from each other.

People in town found it amusing when they would see them driving around town in their pick-up truck, sitting close to each other. They rode this way until Federico fell ill and couldn't drive anymore.

Their three boys are grown, educated and gone. They have families of their own, two live nearby and visit Luisa often. One lives in Houston and comes as often as he can. All of them earned college degrees, two in Business Administration, one in Computer Science. The oldest, Freddy Jr. graduated from Texas's Southmost College (currently University of Texas – Rio Grande Valley) and went into banking. He currently works as senior Vice President with *Lone Star Bank*.

Their second son, Javier, worked for *Exxon* and later opened an insurance agency. Their youngest Javier is presently the Technology Director at Los Fresno's High School near Port Isabel, Texas.

Luisa lives alone now as Federico is gone. He passed on several years ago. She lives with the many memories of all the wonderful love filled years she and her husband shared together.

"I admired the wives whose husbands are shrimpers. It's a lonely life, for both the husband and the wife, being apart for long periods of time. I am so happy and grateful that my husband worked at home."

13

TRINE & INEZ CUEVAS

Trine and Pepe

    Trine, short for Maria Trinidad (Trinity) was born in 1946 in the Mexiquito neighborhood of Port Isabel. She knew all the ins and outs of the shrimping business. She grew up directly across the street from the shrimp docks on fish house row. She was awakened every morning to the sound of laughing sea gulls as they excitedly welcomed the new dawn. The joyful guffawing of the gulls was soon followed by the loud put-put-put puttering of shrimp boats bilge pumps as captains emptied seawater seepage from the night before. She went to bed at night with the same reverberation of the bilge pumps as they echoed through every open window of the waterfront neighborhood.

She accompanied her mother and all the other mothers in Mexiquito to head shrimp as a young girl. All her life from early childhood through adolescence and into adulthood was centered around shrimping. She even married a shrimper (Pepe Cuevas). Together they built a thriving family business of shrimping boats with a fish house of their own.

It wasn't easy. After they married, Pepe went shrimping as a deck hand header, worked his way up to rig man and eventually captain. All the while Trine stayed home and took care of the house and kids. They saved their money. They dreamed of one day owning their own shrimp boat. When they had enough saved for a down payment, they looked for and found a boat they liked. They went to the bank, got a loan for the balance and went into debt as boat owners.

Pepe took the boat and with all his determined energy worked it like it had never worked before. Trine was just as determined. She budgeted the money and closely monitored household expenses. She knew how hard her husband worked. She was going to do everything she needed to do on her end to make sure she kept the house and kids healthy, paid the bills and made the boat payments. Many shrimpers buy a shrimp boat but for whatever the reason they do not manage the money properly. Shrimp boats are costly to maintain and operate.

The shrimping industry is an unconscionable business. The strain on the equipment is unforgiving. The Gulf of Mexico is a large body of water. Its winds can whip up to gale force at any time with ten-to- twelve-foot waves that will pound shrimp boats mercilessly.

They paid off their first boat. They mortgaged a second boat and another until they had a fleet of nine. They survived the ever-increasing government regulations that cut into their profits. It seems that every year, bureaucrats came up with one more rule or law telling shrimpers how they need to implement a method that will decrease their catch. Trini dealt with the ever-rising costs of fuel and equipment, the drop in the price of shrimp, the lack and delay of permits issued to foreign workers.

Not long after World War II, Port Isabel had an influx of shrimpers from Louisiana. A group of them made a prospecting trip to the Gulf waters off the southern tip of Texas. The excursion paid off big time. They found gold in the shrimp. The virgin sea bottom off the coast of Port Isabel had never been fished for shrimp before. They immediately returned to Louisiana, packed up the wives, kids, boats and moved to Port Isabel. Coincidentally, Trine was born during that time. So, it's safe to say that both Trine and shrimping came to life together in Port Isabel.

Being around shrimping and shrimpers was all she knew. It was a way of life for her. By the time their children were growing up, she and Pepe were already established and prosperous.

When the time came and the boys were old enough to go shrimping, they were put on boats during the summer. The girls learned the business by observing their mother and father make decisions regarding the maintenance and operation of the boats.

Trine was a full partner in the business. When it came to making expensive decisions, nothing was finalized unless she signed off on it. She took care of their money as well as her crews. She was a mother figure, never hesitating to sit a crew member or their wives in front of her desk to let them know they were doing something that wasn't correct. In the end, her wise motherly intervention was always appreciated.

Although Trine was conservative with their money, she had a generous side. She knew that God had blessed her and her husband. Their many years of hard work had been good to them. When it came to contributing to charitable causes, Trine and Pepe could always be counted on. They generously gave to the church and the church's charities. She raised her children to be the same, making sure they had a strong foundation in the teachings of Jesus Christ, and the blessed Virgin of Guadalupe.

Their beautiful daughter Inez, was as they say, "a chip off of the old block." After graduating from high school, she went to work as a bookkeeper with *Bodden Caddell Trawlers*. She was under the tutelage of Ms. Ida Rivera who kept books for dozens of boats and mentored many girls coming out of high school into the workforce of keeping books for shrimpers. After learning the shrimp boat bookkeeping side of things, she went to work for a local bank. She started as a teller, moved to cashier and later to the money loaning part of banking.

After learning how to keep books and banking, she worked for the family shrimping business. Although her mother was well versed in the money management part, Inez brought with her a knowledge of banking and accounting as well as bookkeeping. Like her mom before her, she too was frugal with the company`s money.

They bought real estate properties and more boats. At a relatively young age in her thirties, she and her husband Joe Martinez had bought three boats of their own. Like her mother, Inez married a shrimper. Joe Martinez is the son of Israel Martinez, another lifelong shrimper. Inez was born to be a shrimper wife and boat owner, following in the footsteps of her mother. Inez was a strong, driven sidekick of the operation.

She was elected to the Point Isabel School District. She wanted to be an active participant in sustaining a quality education for children. She worked hard to raise it to a higher standard.

Inez left us way too early. She became ill with breast cancer. She fought to the end. She never stopped fighting. Her perpetual smile never left her face no matter how sick she was. She continued with her church and civic responsibilities. She was forty-two years old in the prime of her life when God called her home.

The family built a shrimping legacy that still endures. Many shrimping companies have closed operations. Cuevas trawlers continues. They left it in the able hands of E.J. (Edward Junior), fourth generation shrimper who runs and operates the boats, Captain Edward Sr. third generation mariner admits that all he wants to do is be out on the Gulf catching shrimp. Joe runs and operates *Los Tortugas* restaurant seafood market and Lisa, the youngest, is a banker.

"She (Trine) was always smiling. She ran the company by being cordial to everyone, but using tough love whenever necessary," E.J. laughed at the memory. "What she said was law and we all knew it. She was the matriarch who gave the final okay to Pepe and everyone else."

"She was a devout Catholic and a product of Mexiquito. As a mother, grandmother and owner, she treated everyone the same. I think she learned great management skills as a young girl. She and Pepe were partners and they made decisions together."

Trine and Pepe had four children. Lisa, the oldest lives in San Antonio. Edward, Jr is a shrimper and also E.J.'s father. Joe and his wife own *Los Tortugas Restaurant* in Port Isabel. Inez passed away from breast cancer a few years ago.

"Inez was the enforcer. She helped Trine and served on the Port Isabel School Board before the cancer took her," E.J. proudly showed us her photo.

They all have a job to do. That job is to make sure that "The shrimp you eat today, slept in the Gulf of Mexico yesterday."

14

BEATRICE FLOYD HOLLAND

Beatrice (affectionately known as Bea to the Anglos and Boitice to the Mexicans) was born in Point Isabel, Texas in 1915, to Mariano Garcia Holland and Refugia Perez Holland. Mariano's mother Maria Santos Garcia Holland was a descendent of Don Rafael Garcia, rancher and landowner of El Fronton de Santa Isabella, present day Port Isabel. She was the oldest of thirteen children. When she was born, the population of Point Isabel, as it was known at the time, was between two to three hundred. She attended school in a school building administered by a handful of teachers with less than one hundred students.

Bea was born to a life of surf (the pristine beaches of Padre Island), commercial fishing and public service (her father served as a United States Coast Guardsman, school board member and constable in Port Isabel). When she was four years old her father Mariano, a coast guard surf man stationed at the Brazos Santiago Coast Guard Station on Brazos Island, Padre Island, was heroically awarded the Coast Guard Life Saving Silver Medal. He and other surf men bravely plunged their surf boat smack into the torrent wind and dangerous waves of a hurricane pounding Padre Island and Point Isabel. It was the hurricane of September 16, 1919. They rescued the eight-man crew aboard a sinking Cape Horn Schooner.

After graduating from high school, she worked for various fish houses as a bookkeeper. Her father had become ill and unable to fully support the family. So, it was up to Bea to step up and become the bread winner and main financial provider for the family. She also became the one to go for advice and guidance. Her introduction to the world of business as a bookkeeper helped her learn how to save and invest her money. After making sure her siblings were fed and clothed, she saved whatever money was left over. She purchased a rental property, saved her money from that and purchased another and another.

Working in fish houses allowed her to learn and find out when a shrimp boat became available for sale. The *Dough Boy* was for sale. She bought it. Its purchase back in the 1950s arguably made her the first, or if not the first, certainly one of the first women to own a shrimp boat in Port Isabel. Research did not find another female boat owner during that time. Shrimping was a man's world but Bea thrived in the business. She had developed a good understanding, as well as an excellent reputation among the men as a knowledgeable bookkeeper and businessperson.

Whenever the boats came in with lots of shrimp that needed heading, Bea was one of the person's boat owners contacted. She knew how to get people to the fish house to head the shrimp. She would go to her old neighborhood of Mexiquito, round up people and bring them to the docks.

When boat owners and captains were a man short of a full crew, they went to Bea. She could always find the man they needed. Bea also applied for, completed and acquired work visas and legal residency status for Mexican immigrants who came to Port Isabel.

She was an early pioneer in the Laguna Madre area, empowering women through education, business and the workforce. She was cofounder of the local chapter of the BPW (Business and Professional Women). She strongly believed that women should get a good education and get involved in the world of business, semi-professional as well as professional work. She ran for and got elected to the local school board. Persons who wanted to get elected to local public office came to Bea for her endorsement. She had a large extended family and was beloved by everyone in the community. So, whenever county officials wanted to get elected to county wide office, they made it a point to visit Bea and ask for an endorsement. The same thing happened with statewide as well as national candidates.

Bea married late in life. Before she decided to marry, she stayed by her parents' side, making sure her younger siblings were taken care of. She made sure they all married well or got a good education. She sent some of her sisters, the younger ones, to Villa Maria, a private Catholic school for girls in Brownsville. She did the same for her younger brothers. They attended Saint Joseph Academy, a Catholic school for boys in Brownsville. When the younger sisters graduated from high school she sent them to Business school in Beaumont, Texas and the boys attended local colleges.

It was not uncommon to find a family in need living in Bea's house until they were able to sustain and support themselves. Families with too many mouths to feed often brought one of their children to her. Bea would take the child in and care for it until the family got back on their feet.

She shared and helped however she could. After all her siblings were grown with lives and families of their own, she moved from the family homestead in Mexiquito to the community of Bay Side (now known as Laguna Heights). Many of the families that lived there did not own an automobile. Laguna Heights was about three miles from Port Isabel. They regularly came to her during a medical emergency as well as non-emergency for transportation to the doctor or other appointments. No one was ever turned away.

She worked on people's income tax papers, she sold Avon Products, she notarized legal papers and was always looking for her next real estate deal.

When the Federal Government brought the Early Childhood Education Program (Head Start) to Port Isabel, Bea was one of the principal people to help make it happen. She attended Texas Southern

University in Houston and studied to be an early childhood education teacher for Head Start.

Bea never had any children of her own. She was too busy caring for other family's children.

All her life was devoted to looking for and working at making life better for her community. The legacy Bea left behind is a thriving community through her involvement in the shrimping industry, empowering women through the Business and Professional Women Organization, education, and unselfish charity work.

15

YOLANDA CANTU GALVAN

Yolanda grew up with a history of shrimping in the family. Her mother (Pilar Cantu) had worked as a net maker and Yolanda, like most of the youth in Port Isabel, headed shrimp in the fish houses during her high school years. When she and her husband Johnny (a shrimper) got married she thought she understood what to expect being the wife of a shrimper. But it wasn't until they were married for a while that she found out the reality - the long separations, the disproportionate time of being the sole caregiver to the children and the ever-present worry for her husband's safety.

She married a man who loved shrimping. He started shrimping with his father during the summer months when he was in his teens. Like many of his peers, he was put on a boat and sent out to sea for the summer. Johnny had three older brothers. They all went shrimping during the summer as well. His father liked having his sons fishing with him.

So, when school let out for summer, the boys all knew they were going out on the boat until it was time to get ready for the fall term again. Their father especially liked the fact that he didn't have to worry about having to look for a crew. He had a ready-made crew in his sons. Better still, they were all experienced workers. In them he had a rig man and all the headers he needed. He also had his regular rig man that fished for him year-round. So, when the shrimp run started, the rig man was happy because he had extra help. They could catch as many shrimp as the captain wanted. With him, Johnny and his three brothers, they were able to head every shrimp themselves. They didn't need to come into port for the headers at the fish house to head their shrimp. By working this way, they kept more of the money. The boys were experienced and knew their way around the boat. The more hands on the back deck heading shrimp, the more money the rig man made.

As soon as the nets were brought up after a trawl and the catch hit the deck the boys jumped right in and began heading the shrimp. Meanwhile the nets were quickly returned to the bottom of the Gulf for more shrimp. They had five pairs of hands working while most boats had two maybe three. The Galvan boys had them beat hands down.

Most of the money they earned went to Mom and Pop. They did get to keep some. That's what they used to buy their school clothes, shoes and supplies.

Johnny continued shrimping after high school. In time he and Yolanda bought a boat, the *Julissa Ann,* named after one of their daughters. He was the captain as well as the owner/operator.

Over the course of Johnny and Yolanda's twenty-six-year shrimping career, Yolanda took on a dual role. She went shrimping when Johnny needed her help on the boat. She was also a full-time wife, homemaker, and mother raising six children. She stayed active with her church and school activities. She took on an activist role in political issues pertaining to the industry.

They worked their boat for many years. Like many other one boat families, they tried to stay in the business. Unfortunately, the escalating costs of operating a shrimp boat made it impossible to keep their heads above water. Virtually every dollar they made went back into the boat's maintenance and operation. There was no longer any profit. One boat families sadly became a thing of the past. The only shrimp companies who were able to survive the high costs of operating shrimp boats were companies who had at least three boats. Even those companies struggled to stay afloat. Yolanda and Johnny sold their *Julissa Ann.*

Yolanda spoke of the loneliness she endured. It was especially difficult at night when the kids were in bed and the house was quiet. "I admit I cried times but never in front of my children. I knew they missed him too. Often as I laid in bed alone, I would stare into the cold darkness of our bedroom unable to sleep. Tears rolled down my face to my pillow as I lay thinking of Johnny. I missed him very much. I needed him home with me. The only thing I could do was pray. Prayer helped me get through many lonely nights. I would send my thoughts and love his way.

"Many times, I would hear my children's whimpering cries. It broke my heart to hear them whispering and sniffling consolations amongst themselves. Hearing their cries triggered an uncontrollable flow of more tears. I don't remember how many times I had to turn my pillow over to its dry side when my kids were crying for their dad's safe return. It hurt, but at the same time it warmed my heart to hear them pray."

"Every time he left, without fail we had to prepare ourselves for the long separation the day before. It started with a big hearty breakfast, followed with a trip to the grocery store. We would buy a train of shopping carts filled with groceries. Most of the groceries were for the boat's crew. The rest were for the house.

"After the grocery store, we went to the boat. The crew loaded and stored everything. The kids loved going to the boat. It was an adventure for them. They enjoyed playing in the cabin and wheelhouse pretending they were out at sea shrimping."

"Once the groceries were stored. Johnny had one last meeting with his crew. He gave them their final instructions for departure the next day. After that, we would spend the rest of the day and evening together. It was our family time before Johnny left."

"On the day of his departure we all went to the dock to send him off with farewell hugs and kisses. As soon as the boat pulled away from the dock we got in the Suburban and drove to the jetties to wait for him. Not long after parking and walking to stand on the jetty rocks he sailed by. We waved and cheered our farewell goodbye with both joy and sadness."

"He would be at the helm when the boat came into the jetties. As soon as he saw us standing on the rocks waving, he blew the boat's foghorn, letting us know that he was seeing us, too. He would hand over the wheel to his rig man and come out the port side door of the wheelhouse to wave and blow kisses to us."

"We loved it when he fished close to shore. The kids liked going on the beach to look out at the fleet circling. They went north, up one way and then turned back. The night lights of all the boats fishing back and forth made it look as if there was a floating city just off the beach."

The kids liked to play at being able to tell which boat was the *Julissa Ann*. Every time they thought they identified her, they would shout out, "Look there's the *Julissa Ann*. We took sandwiches, sodas and chips. We turned it into a fun time. It was a way of taking away some of their sadness of not having Johnny home. We stayed there most of the day and even after sunset until it got dark. We stood there on the beach looking out at all the many pretty lights. We saw white, green, red and blue lights bobbing up and down. It looked like a drifting city moving north and south. We didn't know which lights belonged to which boat but we knew they were all our boats.

"We weren't the only family on the beach. Others came out to see the floating city, too."

"We prayed every day for his safety and for a good trip. On stormy days, we prayed longer."

Childhood injuries happen in every family. Yolanda and Johnny's kids had theirs. As is always the case with shrimpers when their children have accidents, fevers or other childhood illnesses, it happens when Dad is shrimping. Mother has to deal with it. "There were times when Johnny was out shrimping." Yolanda remembered. "One of our daughters was choking on something she had put in her mouth. Another time I had to take one of the boys to the ER for stitches. He fell when he was playing outside in the yard and got cut.

In between emergency room and doctor visits there were many bumps, minor cuts and bruises. I can't count all the bottles of rubbing alcohol, iodine, Vicks rub, boxes of cotton balls, swabs, bandages and band aids large and small I went through. You learn to become a nurse." She laughed.

"When Dad came home, he spoiled the kids. I was always strict. But when he was here, he gave them anything they wanted. He loved to take them shopping for new clothes and shoes. We took them to restaurants, movies and other fun places. He wanted to make up for all those many days and weeks at sea."

When Johnny was short a crew member, he took Yolanda shrimping. They left the kids with her mother Pilar and off they went. The need for her to fill in for an absent crew member didn't happen often, but she was always there to help. She didn't like leaving the kids. It was hard enough for them when Johnny was gone. Not having either parent for days or weeks was even harder. "But sometimes it just couldn't be helped" she said.

The hardest part of going shrimping for Yolanda was not the work. She could handle it. It was not being there for the children. It's difficult enough as it is on the kids with dad gone for long periods of time. But when she went shrimping too, it was a double whammy. "My mom was a great caregiver and took really good care of them. The kids love her and liked staying with her. But it wasn't the same. My heart ached for them the whole time I was gone. The bond between a shrimper mother and her kids is special because she is the only parent at home most of the time. She tends to overcompensate. She wants to make sure she is handling her parenting role adequately as both mother and father. Not being there was what hurt Yolanda the most.

"He couldn't find a header and he promised me we'd only be out two weeks. Those two weeks seemed like forever. I thought of leaving the kids constantly. I agreed to go but told him I'd do the cooking and cleaning so he and the rig man could take care of the shrimping. I ended up helping with the heading, too."

The thing I remember the most about being out there was the water. There was water all around me. No land just water and the constant non-stop noise of the engine and the winch. Boats are very noisy.

"One night when Johnny had been working for twenty-four hours without rest, he asked me to take the wheel so he could take a short nap. He told me to wake him when we reached a certain coordinate. It was pitch black. I couldn`t see anything in front of me. I carefully watched our position like he told me. We reached that certain point where I was supposed to wake him up so that we could turn back around. I called him but he didn`t wake up. I kept calling him. He was dead to the world. The rig man was dead tired too. He couldn`t hear me either. I kept going.

"A short while later, out of the blackness. I see a light coming straight towards us. The light kept getting bigger as it came closer and closer. I tried again to wake him up, but he didn't move. I could now see that it was another boat and it kept getting closer. The other boat wouldn't turn away. I was scared. I started to panic. Johnny and the rig man wouldn`t wake up! I thought for sure we were going to crash. I didn`t know what to do. I kept going straight hoping the captain of the other boat would see me and turn. He never turned. Maybe he was asleep too. Finally, the boat passed by on my left side. It barely missed us. The boat was so close I could see the man sitting in the captain`s chair. I saw that he was asleep at the wheel. I breathed a big sigh of relief when he went by without hitting us.

"I kept going straight for the rest of the night and into the morning.

When the sun came up Johnny finally woke up. He came to the wheelhouse, looked at the coordinates and saw that I was way off course. He asked me why I didn`t wake him up.

"After he turned the boat around to get back on course and pick up the nets to head the shrimp, we saw two boats. Their nets tangled to each other. He said, 'See that? That`s what happens when the people steering the boat are not paying attention.' I told him I was paying attention. 'Those fishermen lost their nets and their catch. Thank God that hadn't happened to us,' he said. "I told him about the boat that kept coming at us and didn`t turn. About how it nearly hit us and how it came so close to us that I was able to see the other guy sitting in the captain`s chair. I told him the boat came so close that I saw the other guy was asleep too. He couldn`t believe that we almost had a boat wreck. He apologized and promised never to leave me alone at the wheel again." "Two weeks passed. I was ready and excited to go home. Johnny had told me it was going to be a two-week trip. It didn`t happen like he had said. We didn`t return home. We were catching lots of shrimp and he didn't want to leave. I was disappointed but I understood. It would be twenty-four days before I saw my children.

"I found out how lonely it gets out at sea for all those many days and nights. I asked Johnny to take one of the boys with him to keep him company. He took Junior, our five-year-old son, a few times after that. Junior actually liked it. Johnny kept him by his side always. They slept in the same bunk. When Johnny was in the wheelhouse steering the boat Junior was right there sitting next to him taking it all in. He was a good little crew member. He obeyed everything Johnny told him to do. He paid close attention, learning everything Johnny taught him. The most important thing he learned from Johnny was how not to be a shrimper. Johnny always made sure to tell Junior to stay in school and go to college. I will always be thankful for that."

"The scariest thing Johnny went through was a hurricane. He was running to safe harbor from Louisiana to Galveston. Johnny knew the storm has headed in that direction. It was reported that the storm was going to hit Louisiana where he was fishing. He needed to get away from there. So, he tried to outrun it. A few hours from Galveston the storm caught them. It was a rough several hours, Johnny said. but he brought the boat in, and the crew was safe."

"There was another time when a storm was coming. We were in Port Mansfield, Texas. I was with him. We needed to get out of there and bring the boat to Port Isabel. When we left Port Mansfield, the water was rough. The waves were big and came at us from all directions. Some of them crashed over the bow and cabin. When we got to Brazos Santiago Pass, we could barely see the jetties. Johnny brought us in. We made it safe and sound. Thanks to God."

Yolanda took part in the Texas Shrimp Association's fight against the implementation of the TEDs. At nine years old Junior got involved in the fight as well. During a public hearing on TEDS in Port Aransas, Texas. Junior, inspired by his love for his father's way of life, as well as all the rest of the shrimpers, summoned the courage to stand before a panel of grown men and spoke. He told them how he felt about the TEDs. He told them that even though he was only nine years old, he was a shrimper. He had been going out in the Gulf of Mexico, with his father since he was five years old. During his time shrimping he had never seen a turtle brought up in their nets. Another time, at another hearing, this time on South Padre Island. Junior spoke to the panel again. He wasn't alone. This time one of his sisters stood with him. Once again spoke against the TEDs. But the panel of government officials had already made up their minds. "They were having the hearings just to hear us out. So, they wouldn't be accused of not listening. They did sit there and heard us speak one after the other. But they didn't listen to a word we said. They listened instead to the people who did the study on the decline of sea turtles. The ones that said the shrimpers nets were killing the turtles."

"As far as injuries are concerned Johnny was lucky with all his many years in shrimping. The worst injury he suffered was to one of his fingers."

He had some interesting experiences that Yolanda shared. "Once when Johnny brought up his nets at the end of a drag, he saw something in one of them. He had never seen anything like it before. The net was still dangling a few feet off the deck. He went up close for a better look. At first, he thought maybe it was a big shark or hopefully a giant grouper. If it was a grouper, we would have a year's worth of fish for the freezer.

Upon closer inspection. It was neither shark nor grouper. It was a big metal object. He ordered his rig man to lower the net to the deck. He untied the knot at the bottom of the net to open it. To let the load of shrimp, fish and the large metal object empty onto the deck.

After clearing the shrimp, fish and crab away from the object, they tied and secured it to the rear railing of the boat, away from everything and everyone. The crew headed the shrimp, stored it away in the freezer and cleaned the deck.

Johnny radioed the Coast Guard and described the object to them. They told him to come back to port and bring the object with him. As it turned out the big metal thing happened to be a live bomb! "When they came home, the bomb squad came on board and took the bomb. They evacuated the port.

"They told him to wait while they unloaded the bomb. They took it out to a little sandbar in the Bay, dug a deep hole, buried it and then exploded it. I was at home. The explosion shook all the windows of our house.

"Another time during a cold, rainy Christmas Eve, we were at home with the kids. Everyone was in the Christmas spirit. We were making cooking and eating tamales and having a relaxing time with the kids. Johnny received a phone call from someone that the boat was not at the dock.

Johnny had not told me that, in the spirit of Christmas, he had let a homeless man stay and sleep on the boat. The night was cold, and Johnny wanted to give the man a warm place to stay the night. He also left some food for him to eat. Well, much to our surprise, the homeless man decided that he was going to go for a boat ride. He started the boat's engine, untied it and headed up the ship channel towards the Port of Brownsville. With the help of helicopters and men with horses, the Coast Guard was able to lower Johnny on the boat. He took the boat back from the homeless man. He brought it back to the dock and tied her up again. The police arrested the man. Instead of spending Christmas Eve nice and warm on the boat, he ended up spending it in a cold jail cell. They released him the next day. Johnny told the sheriff he was not going to press charges on the man. The boat was not damaged. It was Christmas and Johnny felt sorry for the man. It was our most exciting Christmas Eve ever. When Johnny got into the helicopter the kids and I followed in our Suburban. The kids had their heads out the windows waving at their father who was riding in the Coast Guard helicopter trying to get to their boat. They thought it was the coolest thing, seeing their dad up in the helicopter.

"Every time the boat came in from fishing, Yolanda and the kids were right there on the dock waiting for him. Yolanda had a short-wave radio at home. Johnny radioed ahead just after passing Los Brazos de Santiago into the calm waters of the Laguna Madre. He would let Yolanda know he would be at the dock shortly.

"Once the boat was docked. Johnny went to the fish house to get his unloading time. He would unload that same day. Johnny would let the kids get on the boat. They loved playing in the wheelhouse and cabin.

After the boat was unloaded, he got his dirty clothes, locked the boat and came home.

"The next day if there wasn't any school, we all went with him to the boat. The kids played while he and the crew cleaned and did maintenance work. During one of those boat maintenance days, we were all on the boat as usual. The kids were running around, playing and having fun. The sun was high, the temperature hot, the kids had been complaining about the heat and wanted to go swimming. Johnny had told them that maybe they could go swimming after he got done with his work.

He had to bring out the life jackets and tie some life rings and ropes over the side for them to hold on to and climb back on board.

Jamie, the youngest one, heard her brothers and sisters say they were going swimming. Not realizing that she had to wait for her father to bring out the life jackets, hang ropes, a ladder and life preservers over the side, she decided to jump in the water. She had never gone swimming in the channel before. In fact, she was too small to go in the water at all. Only the older kids were going swimming.

By the time they saw her on top of the railing, it was too late. They couldn't get to her in time. My heart almost jumped out of my chest.

I screamed for Johnny. We all ran to the railing where she had jumped. Jamie didn't know how to swim. The rig man, Señor Jaime Castor, who had been fishing with Johnny for many years, made it a point to be extra vigilant when the kids were there. When he saw Jamie was about to jump, he ran to her but was unable to get to her on time. Without breaking stride, he dove over the railing. He went in after her headfirst. He was able to see the splash where she had gone under. The channel water at the docks is not the cleanest, clearest water in Port Isabel. I don't know how he did it. Somehow, he saw her little arms and legs. He reached for her and was able to grab one of her arms. Within seconds of Jamie hitting the water, he was in there too.

All of us ran to the railing looking into the water, frantically yelling and screaming her name. As soon as the rig man popped his head out of the water with her safely in his arms, Johnny threw over a rope tied to a life ring. The rig man tied the rope under Jamie's arms and around her waist. Johnny pulled her up back onto the deck. She got a good scolding. That was the end of the workday and no one except for Jamie went in the water that day. They went home instead to get over the shock. After that scary day, the kids never asked to go swimming in the channel again."

Yolanda is rightfully proud of her children and ten grandchildren. All the children attended college. Her first son, Junior, is a coach in Pharr, Texas. Julissa, the oldest daughter, is a Deputy Sheriff for a county on the East Coast. Jacob is a water treatment plant supervisor with the Brownsville Public Utilities Board. Jamie and Judy both studied culinary arts and are bakers. Jarrett is finishing school at Texas State Technical College.

They sold the boat when Jarrett was born. The expense of operating the boat was no longer profitable. Johnny was still staying out for months at a time. After paying the crew their share, covering the boat`s expenses and repairs, there was hardly any money left over for them. Johnny went to work as a bus driver for Point Isabel schools.

The kids are all grown now. He comes home every day after work. It wasn`t this way when the children were small.

But at least now, Yolanda has a husband who comes home every night. She sleeps a lot better now.

16

RITA ALANIZ GARCIA & EULOGIA VILLAREAL ALANIZ

Rita always wanted to go shrimping. Her father, Uvaldo, owned and captained his own boat *The Robin*. It was a wooden hull, he and his wife Eulogia bought with the money they had saved.

Uvaldo was born in Brownsville, Texas but grew up on the family ranch east of Matamoros, Mexico. The ranch is located on the salt grass ranch land known as La Burrita (female donkey), one of several ranches surrounding El Refugio (ranching commune) on the Gulf of Mexico next to Playa Bagdad on the Mexican side of the Rio Grande.

The same La Burrita is a ranching community made up of several pioneer ranching families who ranched and farmed along the Rio Grande

River on the U.S. Mexico border. Before the Brownville Ship Channel was dug in 1936, it was normal routine for families on both sides of the river to come and go, trade, do business or visit relatives.

In fact, numerous pioneer Burrita families moved to Port Isabel during the late 1800s early 1900s to live and settle in Port Isabel.

Not every member of the families moved to Port Isabel. Some had to stay in La Burrita to work and keep possession of the ranches. During the school year they sent the children to live with relatives and attend school. In the summer the children along with their now Port Isabel cousins would return to La Burrita to help out on the ranch.

Rita belonged to one of those families. Uvaldo Alaniz came to Port Isabel where he learned to work on water, the Laguna Madre first. When he was older, he made the transition to shrimping in the Gulf of Mexico.

His parents stayed and worked on the ranch in Mexico. Uvaldo and some of his older brothers and sisters were sent to Port Isabel, to stay with relatives, attend school and work. Frankly speaking, it was for purposes of work than for school. From a young age, Uvaldo learned to pull, carry and toil like a ranch and farm mule.

After years of going back and forth. Uvaldo grew into a strong, strapping, handsome young man. He met the beautiful Eulogia Villarreal, a Port Isabel girl. They courted and married. By that time he was already a seasoned shrimping rig man. They loved each other dearly. Eulogia was a beautiful intelligent young lady. She graduated from Port Isabel High School in the top ten of her class. She had beauty and brains; he had a strong back and the will to work hard for his wife and children.

The Robin was the name of their first shrimp boat. Whenever he came in from one of his shrimping trips. Eulogia took the kids to the boat. They all absolutely loved *The Robin*. Next to their parents, the children thought the boat was the greatest thing ever.

They were proud of their captain husband and father. He too felt great gratification with the way his life had turned out. He was a family man with a loving wife and children. He found that his purpose in life was to work hard and provide for his family. He was content, fulfilled. He spoiled his wife and children. When Rita asked him to take her shrimping, he said no. Rita persisted. She wanted to know what it was like. She was his first born, the apple of his eye. There wasn't anything Rita couldn't ask for that her dad would not do or get her. She wanted a horse; he got her a horse. She named it Fury after the horse by the same name in the TV show *Fury* in the 1960s. He taught her how to saddle and ride. She became a good rider. She loved and cared for the horse and the horse loved her. She wanted to drive a car at eleven years old. He taught her to drive.

Rita continued her quest to go shrimping. She recruited her mother to join her in her sea voyaging pursuit. Eulogia, like her husband, usually indulged Rita's every whim. They did so because Rita was the ideal child.

She was brilliant in school; she helped her mother look after and care for her younger brothers and sister. She was loving, always cheerful and well mannered.

When she started school in the first grade, her teacher told Eulogia she was referring Rita to remedial level. Eulogia asked why. She knew her daughter. She knew for a fact that Rita was a smart, intelligent girl. Eulogia and the teacher met. Eulogia asked the teacher to justify her decision. "She doesn't know how to speak English," the teacher told Eulogia. Eulogia assured the teacher, Rita, was fluent in English as well as Spanish. The teacher told Eulogia that Rita was not verbal and didn't talk much in class.

Eulogia informed the teacher that her assessed judgement of Rita was wrong. She explained that Rita's quiet, well-behaved manner in the classroom should be appreciated not punished. She assured the teacher that Rita's English speaking skills were just as good as any of the Anglo boys and girls in her class.

Eulogia challenged the teacher to administer whatever first grade English proficiency test they had to Rita. The teacher apologized for her preconceived bias that because Rita was a quiet, well-mannered Mexican American little girl she could not speak or understand English.

After that parent teacher conference and a mother-daughter talk at home after school, Rita remained in regular class with the misunderstanding corrected.

A few weeks after the parent teacher conference, Rita found herself in a different class. Rita's mother was correct. Not only was Rita fluent in Spanish. Her English language was just as good as the English only speakers. Rita was placed high first.

Eulogia made sure that the English language or lack thereof was not going to be a deterrent to her children's educational success. As soon as she and Uvaldo had Rita, they moved out of Mexiquito, and into the side of town where the Anglo families lived. Her children were going to grow up with the better of two worlds. She was going to be the link between her children's American and Mexican culture. They were going to feel right at home with both. They were going to grow up loving, singing, dancing, eating and talking Mexican. And they were going to grow up loving, singing, dancing, eating and talking American.

Rita's shrimping trip finally happened. The crew was composed of Rita, her mother and her father. She was under the impression that the trip was going to be a fun one. Just like the picnic boat rides, they took every year during Shrimp Fiesta, with soda pop, sandwiches and a small queasy feeling in her stomach from the motion of the boat caused by the Gulf swells.

Rita was fine the first few hours out. When they got to a fishing spot. Her father dropped his try net. Minutes later, he found out his hunch was right. He was on top of some shrimp. He dropped his nets for a drag. Eulogia cooked a small meal they ate. After supper Eulogia and Rita washed the dishes, pot and pans and cleaned the galley. Uvaldo was in the wheelhouse steering. Rita and mom joined him.

He sat her in his captain's chair. She felt special. She felt like a royal Portuguese sea princess. Her father stood firm on his stumpy sea legs commandeering *The Robin*. She looked over to him. She couldn't help admire how sure, how confident he stood at the helm steering the boat with his strong hands and muscular arms. She saw her father for the first time in his element. She saw how magnificent he looked.

She examined him head to toe, engraving forever in her memory what a shrimper captain looks like.

He was one with the sea. She could tell he was right where he wanted to be. She realized it by seeing the proud grin on his unshaven face. He wore a pale blue cotton shirt. The top two buttons undone and knotted at the waist. His khaki pant legs tucked inside his white shrimper deck boots.

Her mother stood between them. She balanced herself with one arm on the back of the captain chair, the other on her husband's muscular shoulder. Like her husband, she too was fully attired in shrimper clothing. She wore her white boots, khaki shirt and pants tucked in the boots. Her shoulder- length hair was tucked up under a baseball cap.

Everything was good. The cool, moist, evening sea breeze massaged her face. Her frizzy long jet hair was pulled back into a ponytail. It glistened shiny black, as she combed it back with her wet hands after wiping her face from the occasional Gulf spray that splashed over the bow. Her dark eyes shined bright reflecting the sunny day outside the cabin of the boat.

She listened attentively to her father's coded radio conversations with other captains doing the same thing they were. She concentrated hard, taking in the back-and-forth dialogue coming in off the radio airwaves as she tried to decipher their meaning. She asked her mother what all those code words meant. Her mother told her she didn't know. She would have to ask her father.

As soon as the fading sun began to sink into the western horizon, her father told Eulogia, "Here, take the wheel. I'll be right back. I have to put "the chango" (code word in Spanish for try net) in the water. Eulogia was apprehensive at first. She had never steered a shrimp boat before. "Don't be afraid," Uvaldo said. "I'll put it on automatic pilot. If you see a boat coming towards us yell out to me, I'll come running. It won't take me long."

This made Rita perk up. She moved to the edge of the captain's chair. Her mother was at the helm, and in control of the boat. This was exciting stuff. It was time to fish! "Help me," Eulogia said to Rita. "Look for boats. The light of day is going. It will be dark soon. If you see any lights coming our way let me know so that I can call your father."

As soon as dusk turned dark, and the night sky began to twinkle, they began to see lights appear all around them in the distance. It was as if a bevy of lighting bugs had taken flight in the early summer night.

And just like lighting bugs whose flickering green, yellow, orange light flicker on and off, they found themselves amid floating white, red and green lights, blinking on and off. Luckily none of the lights were coming towards them. They were moving in a big circular parade. They were all going the same way. Seeing the circus of pretty lights meandering at a snail's pace, Rita began counting. She often went up on the roof of her house at night to count stars. She found out that counting lights on the night sea was like counting the stars in the sky.

"Fifty," said Uvaldo as he suddenly popped back into the wheelhouse. "Fifty what?" asked Eulogia. "Fifty shrimp in the chango. Time to turn back." "Fifty is not that many shrimp, Dad," Rita said.

"It is to me, Mija. It means we're on top of a small spot of shrimp. Got to go back and get them."

Uvaldo took the wheel from Eulogia, yanked it from automatic pilot and began to turn port side. He asked Rita to stand in front of him to help him spin the wheel. She moved her hands in unison with his. She felt the tilt of the boat as it turned. She didn't know how many degrees the boat was leaning to the port side, but she had to bend her knees, brace and push back on her port leg to keep from flying up against the side wall of the wheelhouse.

Uvaldo maneuvered back and forth a few more times on top of the shrimp spot, checking the chango each time. When the count got below twenty. He said, "Okay girls, time to get to work. Time to pick-up the nets." He moved *The Robin* away from the others fishing nearby. He made sure no one was in front, back or to either side. He was the only experienced shrimper on the boat. It was his wife and daughters' first time fishing. He was going to bring up the nets by himself.

He put the boat wheel back on automatic pilot. He told Rita and her mom to go to the stern of the boat with him. After making sure his lady crew members were standing in a safe spot away from the winch cables, he winched up one net, opened it and dumped its contents on the deck.

Rita's and Eulogia's eyes opened wide. As soon as the load hit the deck, they immediately began to skip and hop back away from the hoard of sea creatures they were certain were coming at them in attack mode. Bewildered crabs, fish, and shrimp scurried and slithered in all directions. The poor underwater organisms were just trying to find their way back home to the bottom of the sea. Rita's shrimping boots were three sizes too big, but she was sure glad she had a pair on.

The other net came up on deck. Uvaldo placed two small deck stools and a basket between mother and daughter. He gave each of them a small, shorthand hoe and a pair of rubber gloves. "Put them on, sit down on the stool and do like I do," he said. "Time to head the shrimp."

It wasn't long before Rita began to feel sick. She had a queasy feeling in her stomach. The smell of the shrimp and the rest of the catch went straight to her nose. The smell of the sea life combined with the diesel exhaust fumes began to churn her gut. Moments later the sea sickness hit her.

It was also at this same time that Rita got to see what her father was made of. She had never seen him like this. Suddenly, he transformed from regular dad to superhuman dad. He dashed from the back deck to the wheelhouse to set a new course, back to the back deck to work the winch, lift the nets, send them over the side to the bottom of the Gulf for the next drag. All this frantic movement without sitting down. His hands moved with lightning speed as he popped the heads off the shrimp with the greatest of ease, filling the baskets all the way to the top within minutes.

He was captain, rig man, and header, all in one. He was a one-man crew. After the shrimp was all headed, he went down into the belly of the boat, packed the shrimp, iced it down, washed and cleaned the deck, and back to the wheelhouse.

Not long after the first time, Rita was sick again. He suspected that it would happen but hoped that it didn't. He brought her some ice in a cup. He told her to chew and pass it down. It would help with the emptiness in her stomach and keep her hydrated. Rita did as her father said but her father saw she was getting sicker. He told Eulogia to take her inside the cabin, clean her up and lay her on the top bunk next to a window. The cool night breeze on her face would help soothe the sickness. The prone position on the bunk would also help with dizziness and nausea. "Keep giving her ice," Uvaldo said. Eulogia stayed with Rita. She kept a bucket and some wet towels next to her bunk.

Every time Rita needed to throw up, Eulogia raised the bucket to her mouth. She wiped her and laid her head back down.

Eulogia became concerned when Rita began to belch up green bile. She didn't let Rita know she was worried. She told Uvaldo about the bile. Uvaldo came and looked in on Rita. He brought more ice. He asked her how she felt. Rita said that as long as she remained laying down the dizziness wasn't as bad.

He told her, "Just keep eating ice, it will take a while but you will begin to feel better. Stay in bed. Your mother will stay with you, I'll come back later."

Uvaldo told Eulogia to stay with her. "Don't let her out of the cabin. If she goes out, she may lose her balance and fall."

As the sun came up, Rita felt a little better. The dizziness was gone. Uvaldo had picked up the last drag for the night, moved closer to shore, dropped anchor, shut off the engine, raised and set up the tarpaulin for shade. It was time to head the rest of the shrimp. The sudden silence of the motor stirred Rita. She told her mother she wanted to go back out to the back deck and help her father. The bouncy wake of the previous night had become a gentle roll. She made her way to a spot on the pile opposite her father and sat down on her little stool. She picked up a shrimp with one hand and twisted off its head with the other. She threw the headless shrimp in the basket next to her. Her stomach muscles ached a little from the strain of heaving the night before. She kept picking up shrimp, twisting their heads off and throwing them in her basket.

She looked over the pile at her dad. He wasn't picking, he was plucking! His hands were raking through the pile as fast as he could. The sun was climbing the eastern sky. As the sun scalded up the blue cloudless sky so did the temperature. The cool dawn gave way to hot. The shrimp needed to be iced down.

She was amazed at his speed and precision. As soon as he touched a shrimp the head was off and palmed. He did it with both hands equally as fast. He could palm four or five shrimp in each hand before dumping them in the basket and back to the pile for some more.

Eulogia was in the galley cooking. The spicy aroma of chorizo with egg, the sweet aromatic smell of fresh flour tortillas, newly perked coffee had made its way to where Rita and her father were working. Uvaldo shifted into a faster gear. He urged Rita to do the same.

"The sooner we finish heading, the sooner we can ice down the shrimp, clean up the deck, wash up and eat breakfast" he said.

A couple of hours after sunrise, they were done. Rita's father was a meticulous man. Everything had to be cleaned and put in its place before he could rest and say the job was done.

Rita was hungry but her stomach hadn't settled yet. She was only able to eat half of a tortilla taco filled with chorizo and egg. She washed it down with another ice cold 7-up. Both Uvaldo and Eulogia were glad she ate, even if it was only half a taco. It meant she was going to be all right. After breakfast, they all went out on the back deck and sat under the cool shade of the tarp.

They talked about the night's adventure. Uvaldo reported that they had caught a total of four boxes (four hundred pounds) two boxes per drag. "Not bad," he said.

Uvaldo went to the wheelhouse, lowered the volume on the radio, then went to his quarters to rest and sleep. Rita and Eulogia went to the crew's quarters. Rita took the top bunk, Eulogia took the bottom.

They talked about what it was like for them the night before. About how strenuous, loud, slimy and smelly the work is. Rita told her mother she was in awe of her father. He was able to do all the different jobs by himself.

The middle of the afternoon Uvaldo was up. He listened to the radio and conversed over the airways with some of his captain friends. They talked about last night's catch. For whatever reason captains, like fishermen, always add a few pounds to their actual catch when they talk to each other. After a few minutes of that, he went to the back deck and began to ready the nets for the night's drag. Eulogia and Rita were awakened by the back-and-forth chatter of the captains.

Rita went out back to be with her dad. They talked about random things and not so random things like his shrimping job. Eulogia went to the galley to start supper. Rita came back inside the cabin to let her mom know she needed to go to the bathroom. One of the not so random things Rita and her father had talked about was the use of the bathroom. She asked him where they went. Her father told her they went over the side of the boat. Rita found it to be crude, dangerous, and quite embarrassing.

After supper on the second day. It was time to pick up anchor. Uvaldo told Eulogia he was going to need her help doing it. He told her to slowly move the throttle forward a little bit at a time while he worked the winch with the anchor rope to pull it up. Eulogia did exactly as she was told. Uvaldo uncoiled the anchor rope, took it back to the winch, wrapped it around the winch head and pulled.

With the anchor back in its place. Uvaldo set a new course for his next fishing ground. They repeated the same routine as the night before. Rita did not get sick on her second night. She worked the entire night, heading shrimp and resting with a short sleep in between drags.

Not long after they had picked up the last drag of the night, a captain friend of Uvaldo radioed him that he broke down with engine problems. He gave his coordinates, which was only about an hour away from *The Robin*.

Uvaldo set his course to where his friend was. He put *The Robin* on automatic pilot and told Eulogia to stay in the wheelhouse with instructions to yell out to him if she saw any boats in front of them. It was early dawn; the sun was about to break the horizon. He returned to the back deck to finish heading the rest of the shrimp. He went back and forth from the wheelhouse to the back deck to check on Eulogia every few minutes.

They were able to head and ice the shrimp before they reached his friend. Apparently, his friend's boat was overheating, and the captain had to turn off the engine and drop anchor. When they got to the stalled boat, Uvaldo asked his friend if he was able to pick up anchor. The captain said yes. He had let the engine cool. It wouldn't take long to pick up anchor. Uvaldo told his friend that he was going to position *The Robin* right next to his boat. This way one of his crew members could jump over and help with the ropes. He explained that it was him, his wife and daughter on board with him. Eulogia and Rita of course had never seen anything like this before and were fascinated with the process.

As soon as the other boat's crew member jumped on board *The Robin*. Uvaldo quickly spun his wheel away from the crippled boat, pushed the accelerator power forward and pulled away. The other captain cranked up his engine and lifted his anchor. Meanwhile Uvaldo had already explained to the crew member that he was going to reverse his boat close enough so that the rig man of the other boat could toss his heavy cabo rope to him. He told him where to tie it and that he had to do it quickly.

Rita was told to stay in the wheelhouse while all of this was happening. Eulogia's job was to stand just outside of the cabin's rear door. As soon as the crew member got the rope and securely tied it to where Uvaldo told him. He was supposed to signal to Eulogia that the line was secure and move out of the way. Eulogia was then to relay the secure signal to Uvaldo by quickly getting back inside the cabin and yell to him that the line was secure. After that she was to stay inside the cabin, move to the galley and take Rita with her. Once she gave Uvaldo the word that the line was secure, he pushed forward slowly. The line began to elastically stretch expanding to its limit, making popping sounds as it resisted, testing its strength and resiliency. A good rope will hold a heavy pull most of the time. But there are times when it will break.

The recoil of a busted cabo rope is dangerous. A backfire strike from a busted cabo rope will cause serious injury and may even be fatal.

After getting under way with his friend in tow, Uvaldo told Eulogia and Rita to come up to the wheelhouse with him. He told the crew member to monitor the rope from the window of the crew's quarters at the rear of the cabin. The popping, cracking sounds of the rope could be heard all the way to the wheelhouse as it strained to its maximum elasticity.

Rita's nervous eyes darted back and forth from her father to her mother as the tow line was being secured. She sensed it was a potentially dangerous maneuver. Her fears were eased some when her mother joined them in the wheelhouse.

They had been fishing offshore from Port Mansfield when they got the call from the distressed boat about another hour north of their location. That put them six to seven hours from Port Isabel. With a boat in tow, it was going to add another two to three hours to their return voyage.

The rope was holding up. Eulogia asked Uvaldo if it was safe for her to go to the galley and cook breakfast. It was time for it, plus it would help take their mind off the towing. Besides the three of them, they had the crew member from the other boat to feed as well. Tortillas, coffee, bacon, potato and eggs was on the menu.

After the pots and pans were washed and put away, it was time to clean the inside of the cabin. In those days every time a shrimp boat came in from a trip. The entire inside of the cabin was cleaned to a spic and span finish. The floor was mopped, the stove and ice box were scrubbed spotless, the beds were stripped of dirty sheets, the pine walls were wiped with soap and then coated with varnish. The wheelhouse the same way.

After all the cleanup chores were done Rita had a few hours to think about her shrimping trip. She went outside and sat on the front deck behind the bow with her back resting against the outside wall of the wheelhouse. Her long-curled hair was loose and free now, just like she liked it. She had undone the braid her mother had tied to keep it from getting tangled in any of the many ropes, cables or other riggings that constantly swing back and forth as the boat gets tossed every which way by the waves and wind. The cool briny wind, together with the warm sun felt good on her body.

She thought about her father, her captain, her hero. She now knew and understood firsthand how hard he worked to provide for his family. Before this shrimping trip, she always knew him as Dad. A loving father who went shrimping for weeks at a time, came home tired, slept and rested for a day, took the family out to dinner and a movie, spent another day or two with them before leaving again for another shrimping excursion. She had no idea how intense and laborious the job was. Her love, respect and admiration of him rose to another level. She had always been a daddy`s girl.

She reflected on her new understanding of her parents' unconditional love for her. She thought about her father and his work. She saw firsthand how hard he worked out there on the water for days and nights at a time to get her those nice things.

From that day on she promised herself never to take her father's job as a father and a shrimper for granted again.

Her shrimping trip may have only lasted a few days. She looked at her puffy fingers. They were dotted pink from the many pricks and piercings the spikes on the shrimp heads and tails had left on them. She learned the close brotherhood shared by all shrimpers, especially when they are out at sea.

She thought about her mother. About how much she loved her father. About how brave she was to go out on the boat fishing with him. She sat deep in thought, introspectively looking inward, reflecting on her blessings to have such loving parents and how she would be more considerate of them.

Rita had many proud moments in her life before her trip as a deck hand on *The Robin*. But one of the proudest is the time she went shrimping with her father. An experience she still cherishes today and shall forever remain proud to be a shrimper's daughter.

17

CONNIE GARZA

Connie is a rare breed of woman. She is a true-blue real-life shrimper woman. Connie is a header/rig woman on a shrimp boat. She is a fifty-year-old grandmother. Her six children are all grown and married with kids of their own. Not long ago, Connie lost her son to a tragic electrical accident. Being a woman of faith Connie prays daily. She prays before going to sleep after the first drag is put down and she prays again after going to bed again in the morning after the last drag is picked up headed and packed away in the freezer. She especially prays for the peaceful repose of her son.

A single mother, Connie misses her children while she is out shrimping sometimes for months at a time. Her children and grandchildren of course miss her, too. She makes up for it when she comes in after one of her long trips out on the Gulf of Mexico. After cashing her paycheck, she indulges the kids with outings to the movies, restaurants and shopping. "I live by myself," Connie says. "I can't take the money with me. I might as well spend it on my kids."

"Connie is a great crew member and a fast header," according to her Captain Edward Cuevas. He should know, Captain Edward has been shrimping and commanding shrimp boats for more than thirty years. All his many years shrimping has made him one of the best in the business. Captain Edward is the son of the late Captain Jose "Pepe" Cuevas and Trine Cuevas, owners and operators of *Cuevas Trawlers*, one of the biggest and most successful shrimping companies on the Texas coast. Captain Edward could easily stay on land and work off the dock preparing and sending their boats out. He prefers instead to leave that part of the shrimping operations to his dad, mother, sister, brother and now his son E.J. (Edward Jr.). His life is out on the Gulf. He wouldn`t have it any other way.

Captain Edward hired Connie without any experience. She needed a job. He needed a header so off they went. The first trip Connie went on was during a cold, blue Northern with strong, gusting head winds. She was seasick for about a day and a half. "The waves were huge," Connie remembers. "They were coming over the bow crashing against the wheelhouse. After clearing the jetties, we turned north right smack into it. I was a little nervous at first but not scared. I had never experienced anything like it before. I had heard stories about violent cold fronts from my father, uncles and grandfather. But I really had no idea what they were talking about until that day when I went through one myself. Now I know what they meant when they used to say that sometimes a blasting Northern can be more brutal than a Southern squall. The freezing cold gales will whip up Goliath waves making it impossible for the crew to go outside the cabin to work. Not many things scare me anymore. I have been through a lot of hardships in my life. I have faced death straight in the face and survived. I have seen and experienced personal tragic death right in front of me. That cold front, my first one out there, lasted five days. They were two of them." As soon as we cleared the first one, the next came blowing in right behind the other.

"I can head shrimp as fast or faster than most guys. I'm at a point where I can fill two to three baskets an hour. The more shrimp we catch the faster I get. I love it when we bring up full nets. Covering the deck with shrimp means more money for me. I`m not afraid of the work. I am physically strong and can hold my own with any man out on the boats. I'm learning to be a rig man. It`s only a matter of time; I hope that when am ready, Captain Edward will give me the opportunity. He's a good captain. He looks after and takes good care of his crew, he treats everyone the same. Safety is first with him. He has seen a lot and knows of many other men who have gotten injured and even died because of carelessness on the boats. I love shrimping. I see myself doing this for a long time."

"When crew members on other boats first saw me out there shrimping, they were surprised to see a woman working like them. Without a doubt this is definitely a man's job, a man's world. But I have proven myself. The men respect me. Up to now I have not had any problems with anyone disrespecting me or trying to take advantage of me because I'm a woman. I give thanks to Captain Edward for that. He makes sure no one steps out of line. I think you know what I'm talking about."

"It also makes a difference on how I come across as far as being a woman out there. I make it clear from the beginning that I am out there to do the same job they are there to do, nothing else. I love to cook. I learned from my mother. She taught me well. I can make any kind of fresh homemade tortillas, but the guys prefer the flour ones mostly. I cook delicious stews, Mexican rice, sopas, fideo, caldo, fried chicken and all kinds of other foods. You name it, I can cook it. I especially like to cook fresh seafood out there. We get the best of the best. We have our choice of the biggest shrimp, the freshest fish, squid, and other things that come up in the nets."

"Oftentimes when we have been out for many days and the long haul begins to get to us, the guys get kind of cranky. When I see this happening, I conjure up an especially tasty meal. Men always feel better and calm down after a good home cooked meal."

"The Gulf of Mexico has become my home away from home. I feel at peace when I'm out there. During my down time, when we are anchored out, and the guys snoring away, and the boat is just floating in place slowly rocking back and forth, I like to go out on the back deck, sit and pray. I look out to the horizon and admire the ocean. I think about my children, my mother, my brothers, my sisters. I pray that they are all safe. At night, I look up at the stars and let my mind wonder into its vastness. I love the feel of the night's moist breeze on my face. I love the sounds of the sea. Every day and night I hear the same familiar sounds. I love listening to the sea gulls squawking overhead for a morsel and the sound of a fish or dolphin breaking the surface of the water that has come up to look at my world for a moment."

"I love and look forward to hearing new unfamiliar sounds, sounds I have never heard before, sounds... that will forever be engraved in my memory. I like the smell of the sea, the salty taste as I breathe. I even like the rusty smell of the boat. What I don't like is the smell of the men. Shrimper men for whatever their reason or excuse, don't take baths very often when they are out on a boat. I don't say anything to them about their bad smell. They work hard. If they want to go without bathing, I'm okay with it."

"At this point in time, I don't see myself doing any other kind of job. I understand why men who love the sea want to return to it as soon as they can. Me personally, after we come back from a long fishing trip, a week later I'm ready to go back out again. It's a different world for me out there. My stress level goes down. I feel tranquil. I leave my land problems behind."

"When I told my mom, I was going shrimping, she almost had a heart attack. She thought I was crazy! She said shrimping was a man's job. My father was a shrimper, my uncles were shrimpers, my grandfather was a shrimper. She had heard about all the bad things that happen on shrimp boats. She also knew about the kind of men that go out on these boats."

"She was not only afraid that I could get hurt or fall overboard. She was also afraid of what the men could do to me. I told her not to worry. She raised and taught me right. She and dad taught me how to take care of myself. This was something I wanted to do, and I was determined to do it. My children are grown with lives of their own and now it's time for me to do what I want to do."

"I have fished all the Texas coast, the Louisiana coast, Mississippi, Alabama, the Florida Gulf coast all the way down to Key West. I have crossed the Gulf of Mexico from Texas to Florida, filled and packed freezer bins to the top with over 400 boxes of shrimp and crossed back again sailing heavy in the water from the weight of the shrimp."

"I have been out on the Gulf of Mexico during a storm when the waves have been so big that we have come inches away from being flipped over. Luckily, we were able to make it to Key West, and wait for the storm to pass. I have been out in the middle of the same Gulf when the surface of the water is as calm as can be, as smooth a mirror."

"I have had a close encounter, a near miss with a giant cargo ship. Once off the coast of Florida, a submarine boat came up to the surface out of nowhere right in front of us. Captain Edward had to quickly steer our boat away to prevent it from hitting us. We thought for sure it was going to hit us. It came really close. Then suddenly just as it appeared. It went back under and disappeared again. I don't know what kind of submarine it was or who it belonged to. All I remember is that it was big and long and scary. We don't know if they saw us or not. We never saw it again after that."

"I have diabetes, so I must take good care of myself. I watch what I eat. I try to eat more fish than other foods that are not good for me. I take extra care of my feet and hands. A foot injury could be the end of my shrimping career."

"I rub my hands really well with lots of Vaseline before I put on my gloves to head shrimp. The Vaseline helps my hands from getting chapped and cracked. It also helps against the pokes and pricks from the shrimp heads and tails. After I finish heading. I make sure to wash and clean my hands and feet good. I use a lot of medicated lotion."

"I plan to be out on the Gulf shrimping as long as I am physically able. I truly believe that I am at a place in my life where God wants me to be. The day that he sends me a sign telling me that I should be doing something else, that`s when I'll stop."

Connie Garza, a strong woman from Port Isabel, Texas, holds her own alongside the rough, tough men of shrimping. A mother, grandmother, daughter... a true shrimper woman. Not many women can say that. Not many women will do the work she does, to say what she can proudly say. "I am a shrimper."

18

JUANITA GONZALES

Juanita worked for many years for *Bayside Net and Twine*. She began working there in 1963. She stayed with the company until it closed in 2002. Her job, like most of the other ladies, was to operate the twine spinning machines. She was given the option of working in Brownsville after the shop closed. She chose to retire instead. As a young girl, Juanita remembers working in the fish houses. Every time a boat came in, with tons of "head on shrimp," her mother would take her with her gloves, old shoes and dress to work at *Calloway Fishhouse*. As soon as they heard Don Tomas Portugal (fish house foreman) drive by in the company truck honking his horn, they were out the door. They always kept their gear ready.

They had to hurry, everyone did. The sooner you got there, the better spot on the heading table to set up and ready for the loads to come. The preferred places to get were the ones close to the side of the fish house where the boat was being unloaded. These spaces got the first baskets of shrimp, and you could start heading right away.

They joined the other women and their children, the old enough to head shrimp. Juanita fondly remembered her mother's protectiveness during those rushed days. There was a lot of positioning for elbow room. She recalled the competition among the women. Each one had their favorite place on the table, often crossing words if someone else took their spot. She remembered the pay being five cents per pound of shrimp heads. You had to be a fast header and head lots of them.

Shrimp heads don't weigh much more than a feather. They had to bring the weigh master at least one hundred pounds of shrimp heads to earn three to five dollars. One hundred pounds of shrimp heads translates to about five to six hundred pounds of "head on shrimp…" a full day's work. It was extra money for the family during the '50s and '60s.

At five cents a pound for shrimp heads. It didn't take the women long before they realized they were being taken advantage by the fish house and boat owners. It took them years of asking to get paid more for their shrimp heads before the fish houses gave in to their demands. As is always the case, labor and management never agree on wages paid. Labor always wants to get paid more for their work and management wants to pay workers as little as possible. It's always about the bottom line. The less money they pay out the more they keep.

The women didn't have any kind of labor union to speak for them. Shrimpers by nature are independent and almost impossible to organize. For one, shrimping is seasonal and many of the crew are transients. They're here for the season, then move on.

The women may not have had a union to speak for them, but they never gave up their protests for better wages. They also had the power due to their numbers to delay and even stop a boat full of "head on shrimp" from getting their heads squeezed off.

The boats came in with thousands of pounds of "head on shrimp," ready to unload, refuel, load up again with ice and supplies. But if the women did not come to the fish house to head the shrimp, the crew and dock workers were unable to unload. Shrimp requires lots of ice to keep it fresh and not go bad. Tainted or spotted shrimp loses its appeal and value on the market. The price will go down dramatically so a lot of money will be lost.

During the shrimp run, time is money. Every day a boat stays tied up to the dock is a day without money so everyone loses.

When the boat owners and crew pleaded with the women not to stay home when the boats came in because otherwise the shrimp could go bad, the women called their bluff. They held their ground. They may not have had the brawn men do, but they had brains and psychology on their side, and they knew how to use them.

They simply told the men what they always tell them when they want them to solve a problem in their favor. They said, "*Yo no se como le vas a ser, pero a mi me vas a pagar lo mio asi es que figurale.*" Translated into English it means. "I don't know how you are going to do it, but you are going to pay me what I am worth, so figure it out." And so, they did. The men figured out that they needed the women. Without them as their working partners, the industry would not grow as they envisioned it growing.

The fish house owners, captains and crew knew there was too much at stake. In the end, the women succeeded, finally getting paid for the body, the heavier part.

The result was that they justifiably got what they deserved. Shrimp boats came in filled to the gills with shrimp. They got to unload the same day, the shrimp got headed and they went out again for more. The shrimp was processed on schedule, sold on the market, owners and crew got paid and the money started rolling in. Consequently, the shrimping industry boomed, Port Isabel and Brownsville, became the Shrimping Capital of the World. A spin-off of industry-related businesses opened, more jobs were created, and more money circulated. So, it's safe to say that the female workforce involved in the shrimping industry played a major role in its success. They fought for and got the respect they deserved. Because they used their brains, their will and their love for their husbands, their children and their love of the shrimping industry.

Juanita and her husband Roberto Gonzalez raised five children: four daughters and a son. Their oldest daughter, Cecilia, earned a master's degree in education and worked for many years with the Point Isabel Independent School District. She began as a classroom teacher, before becoming a school principal. When she retired as an educator after her many years of service, she was an assistant superintendent of schools. She didn't stay retired long. Shortly after ending her tenure with Point Isabel ISD, she began working with the Texas Education Agency and Region One Educational Service Center, as an educational consultant.

Cecilia Castillo

Her role as consultant requires visits to school districts in the region and provides mentorship for the campus principals. She provides professional development training that enhances the principal's skills and helps them to grow professionally and become better administrators as well as educational leaders.

Besides her busy schedule as a retired/unretired educator, Cecilia decided that her calling and passion as a teacher was still ringing in her ears and burning in her heart. She sought and got elected to the Point Isabel ISD School Board where she has admirably served three terms and has been re-elected to a fourth. The educational welfare and success of the Laguna Madre's children remain one of her most important priorities.

As if the tremendous amount of energy and personal time she unselfishly gives to her school community is not enough. She is also co-owner of a seafood market and restaurant with her husband Joe Castillo.

Together, they opened a small mom and pop seafood store, called *Gulf Seafood* more than forty years ago. With years of tireless work and effort, they grew the small seafood market into a thriving restaurant and seafood market. It is now called *Joe's Oyster Bar and Gulf Seafood Market* and is a favorite dining spot with tourists, Winter Texans and locals.

Joe's Oyster Bar and Gulf Seafood Market has become so popular for their great tasting seafood that they have expanded the business to the Houston area where their son Joey runs the operation.

Juanita's second daughter, Ida, (also interviewed for this book) has spent her career as the bookkeeper for *Bodden & Caddell*.

Her third child and only son, Robert, worked for the Port Isabel and South Padre Island Police Departments. He also worked in Rockport and Ingleside and is now retired.

Her fourth child, Melba, is an office manager.

The youngest, Debbie, lives in LaPorte and is a senior Vice President of a bank there.

19

ROSA BODDEN GONZALES

"All Fred wanted to do was be a Shrimper."

That is what Rosa remembers about her husband Fred. They became sweethearts in high school. After graduation Rosa went to Arlington, Texas. to study Fashion and Interior Design. Fred stayed in Port Isabel and went shrimping. When he wasn't shrimping, he worked at various land jobs in Port Isabel. During Rosa's second year in college, she and Fred got married. They moved to live and work in the Dallas metroplex. Fred went to work for the food store Safeway. Rosa continued her course work earning an associate degree in fashion.

She aspired of finding work in Dallas, in the fashion design market. But her dream of working in the fashion world was put on hold. Fred wanted to move back home to go shrimping. Shrimping was a booming industry; everyone was making lots of money. He convinced Rosa that they should come back home. He would go shrimping, earn lots of money, so she could get a job on South Padre Island. Condominium developers were building high raises on the Island. She could find work designing condo units.

It turned out to be a good move. Fred went to work for Rosa's father.

She found work with an interior design store on South Padre. It was during the late seventies and early eighties. Most of condos being built on the Island at the time were marketed for Mexican buyers from Monterrey. The economy in Mexico was healthy and the Mexicans had expendable income to invest in summer and vacation condos on South Padre Island.

Condos were sold even before they were built. The money was rolling in. The Mexicans were big spenders. They hired Rosa's interior design store to furnish and decorate their condos with elegant furnishings, decorative drapery and accessories. Money was no problem. The more extravagant the better. The Mexican wives made it a point to lavishly outdo each other decorating their condos.

Fred and Rosa were happy. They were doing well. They bought a nice home in a good neighborhood. They welcomed their first born, a baby girl named April. Other children followed. They were involved with church activities, the parent/teacher association at school and all the other regular extracurricular activities young married couples with children do.

They traveled up the Texas coast as a family to other shrimping ports. When Fred went into different ports up and down the Texas coast to re-supply his boat. Rosa and the kids joined him. The kids especially liked the trips. To them it was like a mini vacation. They got to stay in a hotel, play in the swimming pool, eat out and do a little shopping. They were your typical shrimper family.

But as the old saying goes. "All good things come to an end." The Mexican economy took a downturn. The outgoing Mexican Preside, who was finishing his six-year term in office, gave bad news during his farewell speech. The once-healthy peso had lost its strength. It depreciated virtually overnight. Mexicans with money scrambled to get their pesos out of Mexico and into banks in the U.S. The peso had weakened and devalued dramatically. It now took two or three times more pesos to buy a condo on the Island, a luxury they could no longer afford.

As a result, many businesses on the Island suffered. The interior design company Rosa worked for was one of those businesses. There was no more work for her. Luckily, shrimping was still doing well. Fred was making enough money to sustain the lifestyle they had become accustomed to.

Rosa found herself with lots of free time on her hands. After dropping the kids off at school, she began volunteering more of her time at the church. She taught religious classes, helped in the office, the food pantry and other charitable work in the community.

A part-time position became available involving catechist services. The job was offered to her. She accepted. As it turned out the position was a calling to serve the parishioners of Our Lady Star of the Sea Church. Thirty-seven years later Rosa is still working for the parish.

Her many faithful and devout years in the service to God and the church have not exempted Rosa from hardship. Her faith has been tested at times. Through it all, she remains more committed and devoted to her faith than ever.

She survived the most dreaded news a shrimper wife can hear, "Your husband has fallen overboard. We have not found him yet, but the search is continuing."

It was six in the morning 2012. Father Joseph O'Brien came knocking at her door. He told Rosa that Fred had fallen overboard the night before. He told her the Coast Guard and other shrimpers were searching the area where he had fallen. They haven't found him. It had been hours since he went overboard. They believed he had drowned. Her world came crashing down on her.

She knew of other families who had lost husbands, sons and fathers at sea. But she never thought it would happen to her. She asked God why. How could this tragic misfortune happen to her? She thought of their children growing up without a father. She went into shock. The news of Fred's demise spread fast throughout the small close-knit community. Family and close friends rushed to her side offering words of comfort and support.

At around 8:30 A.M. that same morning, she received an offshore cellular call from Captain Polo Cantu. He was calling to let her know he had found Fred. He had him safe on board his boat. Rosa couldn't believe what she was hearing. She knew Captain Polo. She asked over and over if it was truly him or some crazy prank caller. She kept asking because often, when a shrimper falls overboard, especially at night, he is lost forever. Too many things can happen in the blackness of the Gulf waters – sharks for one. The boat is moving away from them. If the captain pulls the throttle to neutral, the boat continues coasting forward. The nets and the rest of the riggings sink to the bottom of the ocean floor. The weight of the rigging will help the boat stop, but it cannot turn around. The crew has to quickly winch the nets on deck. They try to keep sight of the man overboard. They throw lifesavers and anything else that floats at him, hoping that he will swim to one of them or swim back to the boat (if he knows how to swim). Too many times family members report that their loved ones lost at sea after falling overboard did not know how to swim. If the current is too strong and it almost always is, he might not be able to swim against it. Hopefully he can grab on to a lifesaver and wait for the boat to turn back. If they lose sight of him the captain must turn the boat around. Shrimp boats have wide turns; it takes a while for them to make a full circle to the same place.

You would think that knowing how to swim would be one of the Coast Guard's safety inspection requirements for shrimpers, but it's not.

Rosa asked to speak with Fred. Captain Polo handed the phone to Fred. His voice was weak and faint from exhaustion, but it was him. Captain Polo told her they were about five hours away from Port Isabel.

Her prayers had been answered. After Father Joe had given her the shocking news about Fred, she started praying. She pleaded that somehow, some way, someone would find Fred. It was too soon for her to accept that he had drowned. She held on to hope. Maybe by chance, by some miracle he was still out there floating on the surface of water. That's when she received the call. Fred was alive!

She, the kids, immediate family and close friends were at the dock when Captain Polo delivered her husband, safe and sound. He was given a medical exam. Other than fatigue and minor dehydration he checked out fine.

As soon as the distress call went out on the radio that a man had fallen overboard the fleet of shrimp boats that were fishing in the area steamed to where he had fallen over and began the search for him. They tossed lifesaving rings in the water. One of those lifesaving rings is what saved Fred's life. He found one of the lifesavers, grabbed it and held on until he was rescued hours later.

Captain Pat Torres and his crew were fishing on the Santa Cruz when Fred fell in the water. According to him it happened around one in the morning. A fleet of about twenty boats were fishing in the same waters. Captain Pat had gone to his bunk to rest and sleep. It was the rig man's turn to take the wheel. The header joined the rig man on the watch.

Not more than thirty minutes passed. Captain Pat was starting to doze off, when he was startled awake by a sudden jerk and steep left slant of his boat. He jumped out of his bunk and rushed to the wheelhouse. The rig man had spun the wheel all the way to the left. A shrimp boat was headed towards them. It was Fred's boat without Fred at the wheel. Captain Pat knew it was Fred's boat because one of his running lights was burned out. Earlier that night as the boats were passing each other back and forth trawling, Captain Pat had noticed the burnt out light and radioed Fred to let him know about it.

Because many boats were fishing the same area, the header decided to help his rig man by keeping an eye out for boats. Both pairs of eyes were needed. They noticed Fred's boat coming towards them. They waited a few minutes to see if he was going to steer away from them on either side. He kept coming. As the rig man and header watched Fred's boat, they saw what they believed to be a man go over the side and into the water. The rig man got on the radio and called Fred to turn. Also, to let him know they thought they saw a man fall in the water. The boat didn't turn. Fred wouldn't answer. The boat kept coming straight at them. That's when the rig man made his sharp left turn.

Captain Pat got on the radio and called Fred. The men were on the back deck working. They saw the *Santa Cruz*, pass right next to them going the opposite direction. The *Santa Cruz* was flashing their spotlight at them. That's when Fred`s crew realized something was wrong. Shrimp boats are not supposed to come that close to each other when they are trawling. They went to the wheelhouse. Fred wasn't in it. They picked up the radio hand mic to answer Captain Pat`s frantic call. He asked to speak to their captain. The crew of the *Princess Patricia* said Fred wasn`t in the wheelhouse. Captain Pat told them his crew had seen someone on their boat go overboard. He told them to search the boat for him. They looked for him inside the cabin, engine room, the head, the cargo hull. They looked everywhere for him. He wasn`t on board.

Captain Pat directed them to throw their life savers overboard. He said the same thing to his crew. He then told both crews to immediately pick up their nets. As the crews picked up the nets, he began to scan the surface of the water around them with his search light looking for Fred. He radioed another captain friend who was near and told him he thought Fred had fallen overboard. His crew reported seeing someone on the *Princess Patricia* fall into the water.

Within a matter of minutes, all twenty boats that were fishing together began circling the area. The Coast Guard was notified. They immediately jumped into action with their boats and helicopter.

Hours passed; night turned to dawn. Still no sight of Fred. About an hour after sunrise. Captain Polo Cantu and his crew spotted Fred. He was clinging to one of the many lifesavers thrown overboard. He had been in the water eight hours. They brought him on board exhausted, cold and shocked.

Fred tried to continue shrimping. He stayed home for a few weeks spending his days helping his father-in-law on the dock. The *Princess Patricia* went back to work with another captain. After her return trip Fred felt he was ready to take her fishing again. He thought that maybe he had gotten over the shock.

He filled her up with fuel, bought groceries for a forty-five-day trip, hired a crew and went back out again. He wasn`t able to finish the trip. He came back to port before the forty-five days. His mind wasn`t on the job. He couldn't concentrate, couldn't stay focused. He became fearful of the sea; afraid of being out on the water. He feared being alone at the wheel. He wouldn't go on the back deck to use the try net. He was scared that he might fall overboard again. Consequently, he was fishing for shrimp not knowing if there were any shrimp where he was trawling. He became tentative, unsure if he was setting his riggings like he used to. He was bringing up only a few shrimps after his trawls. He was nervous and agitated. His crew began to lose confidence in him. When he wasn't feeling nervous or agitated, he was melancholy. It became obvious to him that he shouldn't be out there so he came home.

His accident had taken a psychological toll on him. He went from a man who was a productive shrimper, who loved the sea, to a man who couldn't do it anymore. It had a devastating effect on him. He had developed some kind of post-traumatic stress disorder.

He went to a doctor. He was diagnosed with depression. Not only was he unable to return to shrimping. He had difficulty keeping other kinds of employment.

Over the years his depression worsened. He was also diagnosed with schizophrenia. Fred was broken psychologically by the ordeal of falling overboard. He struggled with it the rest of his life. He loved shrimping, but the crippling fear of going out there again terrified him. Coping with normal everyday living became increasingly more challenging for him. He began over medicating himself regularly as a means of escaping his trauma. He went into rehab several times, for drug abuse as well as for his psychological illness.

His rehab hospitalizations helped some. He stayed sober for a while but kept going back to abusing his medication. Fred never recovered from his near-death experience of falling overboard at sea. As a result, he lived, struggled and suffered with his emotional disorder the rest of his life.

He died of a brain aneurysm. It happened while he was taking a shower. Fred didn't die at sea when he fell overboard. The traumatic effects caused by the frighting experience ate slowly away at him. He, Rosa and the mental health professionals working with him were the only ones who knew how Fred suffered mentally.

Rosa suffered alongside him. It broke her heart to see him struggle like he did. She tried to help him in many different ways. She prayed with him. She took him to counseling, to intervention rehab; nothing helped. He would be better for a while, but he kept relapsing back into his depression and over medicating.

Fred was the love of Rosa's life. It's safe to say that her survival and stable mental health is a miracle in itself. She attributes her mental wellness and wellbeing to her faith in God. She never gave up hope that one day Fred would recover from his affliction and dependency on drugs. But she also realized that it was because of his disorder that she became the sole caregiver of the family. She had to take care of Fred as well as the children. The entire burden of taking care of the family became her responsibility. Finances and income became a strain. When once, they were a two-income family, now they only had Rosa's earnings to sustain them. Being the strong woman that she is, Rosa learned how to deal with issues related to co-dependency. It was imperative that she remain mentally and emotionally healthy.

She worked hard to make sure that her husband's sickness did not manifest problems with their children.

Fred tried hard to get his life back. He wanted to be the husband he was before his tragedy. The husband who would come home after many days and weeks at sea longing to return to his wife's loving arms.

He wanted laughter back in their lives. He longed to be the life of the party like he was before when his friends and their wives got together after a long shrimping trip. He wished that they could go out again as a group for dinner and drinks.

He couldn't; the laughter was gone. Other than the support and unconditional love and comfort he received from Rosa, who never wavered from his side, he lived in isolation. His psychological depression voided the old Fred. Only he and Rosa knew how he was suffering.

After Fred's death. Rosa began to put her life back together again. She did it by accepting and understanding the ravishes of mental illness. She continued receiving survival counseling. She took continuing education classes and training in religion education to further her missionary call as a catechist.

Today Rosa is at peace with herself. Her children are grown with children of their own and doing well. Her mother Rosita lives with her. Together they live a life of prayer and service to God. Rosa is more energetic and spiritual than ever. Fred is in Heaven. He waits for Rosa there because God has a special place in Heaven for all shrimper wives.

20

ANDREA HANCE

Andrea wears several hats within the industry. For the past eight years, she has served as Executive Director of the Texas Shrimp Association. She also serves as a liaison to several Gulf Coast organizations. Her work entails communication between shrimpers and government agencies.

She and her husband, Preston, bought their first shrimp boat in 2006, and a second one in 2009.

21

THE HOLLAND FAMILIES

Victoria, known as Vita, and her sister, Emma, married Holland brothers, Billy and Uvaldo. Ninfa married brother, Gonzalo. All three brothers made their living as shrimpers. All three wives ran and managed the household. They were responsible for raising the kids, providing structure, administering discipline and all other aspects of keeping the family in line while the husbands were away.

The glue...absolutely. Their husbands and children acknowledged that the family centered on these strong, intelligent women.

"I missed him most on the first day or two after he left. I never wanted him to go back out, so I was sad for several days and would feel sick to my stomach," Ninfa admitted.

"I remember going to visit Ninfa one day after Gonzalo had left," Vita gave Ninfa that I'm-telling-on-you look. "There she was, rolling out big round flour tortillas on the table with tears streaming down her face."

They both laughed. They laughed repeatedly during our interview with them. It was obvious they had many fun, funny times over the years of being shrimper wives. Emma was unable to attend our interview, but Ninfa and Vita enjoyed sharing the stories of their husbands and children.

Their husbands fished during the years when the boats were allowed to fish in the Bay of Campeche for months at a time. Vita communicated with Billy by short wave radio. Gonzalo's boat didn't have a radio, so Ninfa never talked to him.

"We talked almost every night," Vita recalled. "We also wrote to each other and sent the letters with other boats going and coming."

Both women ferried their children (five for Ninfa and six for Vita) to school, extracurricular activities and other events. They are active members of Our Lady Star of the Sea Catholic Church and made sure their children attended mass every Sunday, went to religious classes and became active participants in all the church's holiday programs and celebrations like Christmas, Easter, and the feast day of the Virgin of Guadalupe.

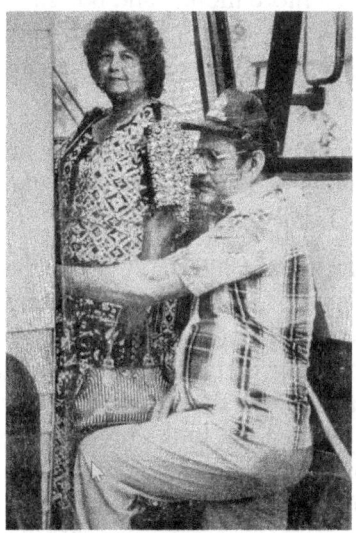

Mr. and Mrs. Billy Holland boarding a bus to Corpus Christi for a National Marine Fisheries Service hearing.

They became involved with Valley Interfaith in the 1980s, making many trips to Austin and Louisiana during the shrimpers' protest of the then-new TED devices. "They stood by their men."

They knew in their heart that the shrimpers were not the main culprits responsible for the decline of the sea turtle population. They didn`t know who or what was causing the turtle numbers to decrease, so they didn't place blame on anyone else. They just knew it wasn`t the shrimpers. Their husbands would tell them that on rare occasions when they brought up a turtle in their nets. The turtle would almost always still be alive. So, they would return it back to the sea.

"It was hard sometimes but we knew what we were getting into when we married shrimpers," Vita said and Ninfa nodded in agreement. The details of any family's existence are in the mundane, day-to-day routines. That includes everything from schooling to sports, resolving family issues as well as doctors' visits, shopping for clothing and groceries. Paramount to every shrimper wife is the ability to successfully manage money. That meant the difference between a happy comfortable life versus a financially burdened life.

Their husbands worked for different shrimp companies through the years. Ninfa and Vita were both able to save enough money to make down payments on their respective boats. The brothers started as partners on one boat. They saved more money and bought a second boat and then a third. After that, each one took a boat and went on their own. Each became responsible for all the record-keeping and governmental compliance that goes along with ownership.

The husbands especially enjoyed their time with the family when they came home from months of hard work. They cherished every together moment they had as a family.

Ninfa and Gonzalo had a pattern. "On his first day home we went shopping for groceries at Lopez's Grocery store in Brownsville. We invited our mothers to come along. It was good for them to get out of the house too. Gonzalo paid for their groceries. After grocery shopping, we would go eat at a restaurant. On the second day, we took the whole family back to Brownsville. It was the kids' fun day. We took them shopping downtown, to the movies and to a restaurant. Brownsville is much bigger than Port Isabel. Main street was lined on both sides with department stores, clothing stores, jewelry stores, movie theaters and restaurants. We would tire the kids out walking all the way up one side of Elizabeth

Street, going in and out of stores and back down again on the other side before the shopping day was done.

The third day was ours. It was our date day. We went to the Majestic movie theater on Elizabeth Street in downtown Brownsville. I liked going there, it was a really nice place. It was our special time to simply enjoy and spend time with each other.

"When they were fishing in Campeche, Billy was never home for the holidays," Vita said. "So, when he came home, it was always family time. We made our own holidays to make up for the ones when he wasn't here. He loved being with the kids. He talked to them, gave them advice and encouraged them in whatever they were doing." He kept his sons away from the boats because he wanted them to get an education and have a better life. He told them that shrimping is a hard life. He doesn't want them to be doing this kind of work. He urged them to stay in school and get an education so they could find a job that paid good money and allowed them to be home with their family.

"We had a great life for many years, but it became much harder when the U.S. and Mexico passed laws against fishing in their waters. Then the government regulations started to get harder and harder on shrimpers. It seemed like everything shrimpers were used to doing, the government passed a law telling them they couldn't do it anymore. They started letting in farm-raised shrimp from other countries. Then the costs of operating the boat began to go higher and higher. By the time we paid off all the bills after each trip there was little money left over for us. Our husbands were working hard and staying out on the Gulf for long periods of time for nothing. It wasn't a good living anymore, so we sold the boats and got out."

Like most mothers, Ninfa takes great pride in her children and grandchildren's accomplishments. After college, her oldest daughter, Hilda, works at Texas State Technical College (TSTC).

Frances, the second daughter, went to college in Beaumont, Texas. She's a teacher for the deaf. She chose that field of study because she grew up with a brother Gonzalo Jr. who is deaf. Her husband is a chemical engineer. His job has taken them to live in different cities throughout the U.S. as well as countries overseas.

Michael is the third child. He currently owns and operates his own business selling and installing hurricane shutters throughout the Valley. His wife, Susana, is a nurse with the Los Fresnos school district.

Gonzalo, Jr attended the School for the Deaf in Austin and then worked at *Blackbeard's* restaurant on South Padre Island. His current health issues do not allow him to work anymore. He lives with his mother in Port Isabel. "He helps me so much," she said.

The youngest, Patricia, also attended college in Beaumont and is a first-grade teacher. She lives in Angleton, Texas, and recently became a grandmother. After raising three boys, she now has a girl in her family.

Vita and Billy have been blessed with six children, four daughters and two sons. Katie, the oldest, owned and operated a childcare facility for many years. She currently lives at the Inverness on South Padre Island.

Junior joined the U.S. Marines after high school. After his discharge he went to work with the U.S. Border Patrol, where he worked until his retirement.

Cindy, the third child, is the family's adventurer. She has traveled all over the world. She has lived in New York and Denver and works for a company that manufactures lids for soda pop bottles.

Henry works as a security officer. He's head of security at *Isla Grande Resort* on South Padre Island.

Sandra was a soldier in the U.S. Army for eight years. After her military service she became a teacher at Garriga Elementary School in Port Isabel.

Annette was in the U.S. Air Force for eight years. She is an Iraqi war veteran. She now works for the Veteran's Hospital in Wyoming.

Vita, Emma, Ninfa, three girls born into Port Isabel pioneer families. They grew up in Port Isabel before shrimping, before it became the shrimping capital of the world, before there was a causeway connecting Padre Island to the rest of the country. They were nourished with lots of oysters, fish and crab from the Laguna Madre (Mother Bay).

They married three boys who were also born to a Port Isabel pioneer family. Together they grew, they married each other. They raised children and grew with Port Isabel and Padre Island. They helped Port Isabel grow into the shrimping capital of the world.

22

PENNY BOUDREAUX LOUPE & KALEI BOUDREAUX

Shrimping is in their blood. Wallace Boudreaux (Penny's dad and Kalei's granddad) began shrimping at the age of fifteen and never looked back. In the 1940s he left Morgan City, Louisiana, with his growing family and moved to the Rio Grande Valley. He bought a home in Brownsville and established his business in Port Isabel. He was a founding member of the *Twin City Co-op*. Later, he and Alvah Galloway, a founding partner, split the business between them. Galloway moved his business to another location and Wallace stayed in the existing location.

"Mom was the heart of the family while Dad was gone. Sometimes he'd come in and leave again the same day," Penny said. Penny was born and raised in Brownsville. Her oldest sibling, Carlette, was born in Louisiana before the family moved. "We had a sister, Charlotte who died at birth. Then my brother Wallace Jr, then me, then Michael who passed away at the age of forty-seven. "Dad employed two master welders, Howard Hebert and Bobby Loupe. I married Bobby forty-three years ago."

We asked about the shrimpers' wives and the loneliness they experienced. Penny shared a story about her brother, Mike, and his wife.

Sometimes she'd yell, 'Don't leave.' Once Mike jumped off the boat and swam back to shore. Another time he jumped off, threw his wife over his shoulder and took her to sea for forty-five days." Wallace's presence is everywhere in the business today, although he passed away in 2016.

"We want to keep his dream alive and continue his work." Both agreed on the importance of doing so. Today Penny is the operating owner of the business and Kalei who grew up in the business and loves it as much as Penny, is in training to follow in her footsteps.

Penny said, "I first worked for Dad, outside on the docks chipping away at the rust, painting, and cleaning boats."

"Dad was the kind of father who didn't need to say much to get his point across. As a teenager I had started smoking and didn't want him to know. One day Dad came by while I was working on a boat and said he'd take me to lunch. When I saw him coming, I immediately laid a cigarette down hoping he hadn't seen it. It was too late. He had already seen my smoke puffs from the dock. He never said a word, but I knew he had seen me. I miss him so much every day.

"My uncle was having a family shrimping trip and my cousin asked me to go along. I thought it was a great idea. I told my mom about it and asked her if I could go. She said I must ask my dad. I did but he said no. I kept begging him and he finally relented when I told him I wanted to see for myself the hard part of shrimping out on the Gulf. I was fourteen.

"I was a header. It was entirely different than I imagined. Nobody realizes what it is out there until you live it. The first three days I was seasick. I couldn't keep anything in my stomach. I got over it and was able to eat and drink without throwing up. It felt good. Then when we brought it in, the first load and dumped it on the deck, we would head the shrimp until the deck was cleared. Then I'd get to rest for a while between loads and we started all over again. It's not really hard. You learn and you get faster. The faster you finish heading all the shrimp the more time you must rest between loads. The hard part is sitting on that little stool for hours. It's back breaking."

"It's amazing how when they open the net up and everything falls on the deck. I remember seeing all those shrimps and thinking 'money, money, money," Penny laughed at the memory.

The header is the lowest-ranking crew member. "I don't remember my hands getting sore like everyone says. I guess I was just lucky. I didn't mind any of the work involved. I made two-hundred dollars for two weeks work."

She made three trips, one with her uncle and two with her husband, Bobby. When asked about working with him, she laughed. "We got along well. I had to work like everyone else."

"I never wanted to work up the chain of command because I didn't want the responsibility of running the boat. The wench scared me to death. I was tiny and I was afraid if I had to work the cable, I'd get tangled in it and end up in the wench."

The first trip with Bobby lasted forty days. On the second trip, Bobby's rig man brought his wife, Wendy. Penny told the following story.

"Wendy wanted to go swimming and had already changed into her bathing suit. Before I could change, Bobby picked me up and threw me overboard, clothes and all. Then he yelled, 'shark, shark.' As I tried to climb the rope, he'd just laugh at me. I couldn't pull myself up. He finally tied knots in the rope so I could climb up. Of course, there really wasn't a shark!"

"I remember a strike at *Twin City* sometime in the 1960s. It seemed like everyone was going on strike around town. Most of the strikers were the women who worked hard in the fish houses. They wanted better pay, and they got it. The fish houses needed them.

"I started working in the office when Robert Bennett was Dad's bookkeeper. He taught me the ropes. I have been running the office since 2006, taking on total responsibility when Dad passed.

"Most of our crews and employees have been with us for years. Our visa workers are from Mexico - they've come back every season for over twenty years."

Kalei said, "I started working in 2015. I'm concentrating on learning the entire business, from the bookkeeping to selling shrimp."

We asked about operational problems she's encountered. "One time one of our boats hit another at sea. Another time a captain got sick, and we had to find a new captain and crew. Those are the kinds of problems that can occur."

Kalei has learned the history of the company and the shrimping in Port Isabel from all the many stories she has heard from her grandfather and her aunts. She knows the captains and the crews and has become friends with many of the customers that she has met in the last few years. Her dream is to keep the business alive and, hopefully someday, pass it on to her children.

Twin City Shrimp Company currently has four boats in operation, but Kalei spoke of the difficulty of finding help, or obtaining visas for the Mexican crew members. Every year is a wait and see thing. We must wait for the government to decide when and how many work permit visas they're going to issue. We're pretty much at their mercy. Locals and other citizens don't want to go shrimping anymore. They would rather work on land. The tourist industry offers lots of jobs for them.

23

Laura Picariello

In 2018 Laura Picariello assumed the position of Marine Fisheries Specialist for Texas Sea Grant. Her responsibilities include the entire Texas coast and encompasses working with both the commercial and recreational fishing communities on issues of sustainability. In working with the Texas Shrimp Association, she assists the shrimpers with installation, use and maintenance of turtle excluder devices (TEDs) and bycatch reduction devices (BRDs).

She also considers industry promotion an important part of her work. She explained that Louisiana and Texas have different processes. In Louisiana, shrimpers sell their catch at the dock. In Texas, sales are conducted through processors.

She spoke of the graying of the industry and the difficulty of bringing young people into the industry. With domestic shrimping only producing approximately eight percent of the demand for shrimp, the hesitation to pursue a career in the industry is understandable. Texas has a limited entry on vessels. No new boats are being built unless one of the older boats is retired out of service. That creates problems for expanding the industry.

Laura pointed out that the Brownsville/Port Isabel market has fewer women than other ports along the Gulf coast. Port Aransas has only one local boat working although a Ft. Myers Florida fleet travels to the port for the season opening. Palacios and Port Arthur are active ports, each a small community like Port Isabel.

Before joining Texas Sea Grant, Laura was a Research Assistant, Technical Programs Manager and then Director of Audubon Nature Institute's Gulf United for Lasting Fisheries (G.U.L.F.), a regional sustainable seafood program designed to focus on Gulf of Mexico fisheries.

24

IDA GONZALEZ RIVERA

"I didn't grow up in the industry, but I've spent more than forty years in it, all working for Jasper Bodden."

Ida manages the office books and record keeping for the business including corporations for each boat (each boat is its own corporation). Her job requires her to continuously multitask. Her boss Jasper is a hands-on owner. He is at the dock every day Monday-Friday taking care of his boats. He is also there on the weekends if he needs to be.

He has made it a point to know the whereabouts of every penny earned and spent. Ida makes sure of that. That's what has made him successful in the business. They have worked together for so long that often they each know what the other one is thinking.

Ida has Jasper's full trust. She has proven her loyalty over the years. She knows and keeps up with all government regulations. Aside from her record keeping and accounting duties, she also handles the temporary visa work permit applications for foreign workers.

Bodden & Caddell currently owns six boats, down from thirteen at the height of the industry in the 1970s.

"One of the major problems today is personnel. We had two boats tied up all season last year because we couldn't get the visas for our Mexican workers. This year, we only have crews for two boats, so we will have four tied up if the visas don't come through. It's tough. We've had eighteen visa workers, and twelve of them have been with us for more than thirty years.

One of the highlights for us is July 15, the season opening. We get together out on the docks, Jasper barbecues while we wait for thirty minutes after sunset. Then the season opens, and the boats head out.'"

Rudy added that it's a special time of year and remembers when the whole town took part. The bishop came with prayers and holy water. They would put him on board a boat and take him to every fish house where he blessed each boat. Then the boat parade began.

The celebrated hoopla of the Shrimp Fiesta Days, with all its gaily decorated boats doesn't exist anymore. All that is left of those merry times are the memories and stories told. For Texans who came later, the stories create a longing to have seen those special times.

Ida worked through the good years when the boats always came back fully loaded with shrimp as well as the time when governmental regulations, foreign imports and operational costs nearly broke the industry.

When asked about the multiple corporations, Ida explained that she is responsible for keeping the records updated for each, assessing operating costs, crew payouts and repairs. She updates Jasper twice a month on each boat's current standing.

"Once there were fifteen or twenty bookkeepers here en Port Isabel. Now I can only think of six of us remaining. They are all sharp, smart informed women. We occasionally get together for lunch to share stories."

When asked about some of the stories, she laughed.

"Oh, we heard stories. One of the best I heard was about a woman who wanted an advance payment for her husband's share from a boat he was fishing on. When she was asked his name, she didn't know. "I don't know what name he's using," she replied. "When asked what boat is he on? That brought a similar response, "I don't know the name of the boat. The same goes for the captain. Needless to say, she did not get the advance."

Ida shared more stories, less unique but typical of the industry.

While the boats were out, if a wife needed money, she asked the owner for an advance on her husbands' anticipated earnings. They had to explain why they needed the money. The owner knew if the husband had okayed the possibility of advances before he left.

"One wife told me her little boy had been injured and she needed money to take him to the doctor. When her husband returned, he explained that she had used the same story the year before when the child had been injured."

"All in all, the wives are special women. Being a shrimper's wife is not easy. The husbands are gone for months at a time. During those many days without a husband and father at home is challenging for the entire family. The wife must attend school functions, such as athletic games, band concerts, elementary school presentations and awards ceremonies without her husband. She is responsible for bringing the children to church and religious classes, as well as any other needs they may have. "I admire them for the responsibilities they willingly assume. We currently have two wives who throw a party with food for everyone when their husbands' boats come in. They are exceptional women."

It's not always been easy for Ida, as a woman in a workplace of men. "I've had a couple guys over the years who threatened me. I've learned to be tough, and I keep a bat and hammer in the office in case I ever need it. However, most of the men have treated me with respect and kindness.

"I can't think of anything I'd rather have done in my life. I've loved being a part of an industry that defined our community."

25

ZELDA SIERRA

Zelda has worked at the *Brownsville Shrimp Unloading Dock* for four years. With her background in banking, learning a new business has been a challenge she's enjoyed.

"My boss, Raul Labin Garcia, had faith in me that I could learn the industry. He owns a boat and we have twenty-two accounts, other owners who unload at our dock. As a bookkeeper I handle the licensing, settlements and bill paying. I believe I have a good relationship with the captains and crews. I like working with people and that is a large part of my job. I enjoy the shrimpers' wives and appreciate the support they give their husbands."

She has found few problems. "Once or twice a drunken header has come into the office, but all in all, the captains and crew members treat me with respect.

Most of her work involves the local shrimpers but during the winter, she has two customers she works with at Superior Seafood in Florida.

When the SBA (Small Business Administration) recently gave loans to shrimpers in need, she filled out the applications for them. In total, she submitted one-hundred-and-fifty applications, most of which received approval.

"Our main problem now is getting workers. Each boat must have a US citizen. That is more of a challenge than people realize. It's difficult to find people who want to work the long, hard trips at sea. Like all shrimpers today, we have been hurt by the reduction in the number of visas issued for migratory workers."

When asked if she has experienced any unusual situations, she spoke of a boat owner who had a crew member die while at sea. "It was my job to take care of the details," Zelda related. "The boat docked in Louisiana, so we had to send someone to take care of the arrangements there while we handled the paperwork to transport the man's body to his home in Mexico City."

Zelda was also involved in the details when a captain who was on drugs locked himself in the head. They called the owner who sent his son out. When he finally convinced the captain to unlock the door and come out, he jumped overboard. Several days later his body was recovered at sea.

She sees each year getting harder for the shrimpers to make a profit but has hopes that the industry survives. "A number of the shrimpers are opening their own outlets to sell directly to the public. I give advice when asked and hope that venture helps their bottom line."

26

THE QUIÑONES FAMILY

The month was May. The year, 1975. Eugenio Quiñones Sr., Maria Elena and six children - Perla, Adriana, Esmeralda, Maria Elena, Magda, and Eugenio Jr. crossed the International Bridge from Matamoros, Tamaulipas, Mexico, to Brownsville, Texas. Like millions of immigrants who came to the United States, before them, they came in search of the American dream. They took up residence in a small three-bedroom, one bath, wood frame house on 26th Street, in the southernmost neighborhood of Brownsville. Before coming to Brownsville, the family lived in the Colonia Modelo, Matamoros, Mexico. off and on for fifteen years.

Four of the children were born in Mexico, (Magda Delia, Esmeralda, Perla, and Adriana). Two were born in Brownsville, Texas, (Maria Elena and Eugenio Jr.).

What is certain is that Eugenio Sr. and Maria Elena made a conscious decision together as parents to immigrate to the U.S. with their children. They brought with them a strong bond and love for each other, as well as a devout faith in God.

They brought with them a vision and desire that someday because of their hard work ethic, they would prosper so that their children would thrive, grow, get educated and become successful citizens in their new country.

Prior to being able to work in the U.S., Eugenio Sr. built and sold chicken cages in Matamoros. After getting their visa permits Eugenio went to work in Houston, Texas. He worked for an aluminum window manufacturing company. Maria Elena found work with a shrimp processing company on Fourteenth street in Brownsville. She traveled to and from Matamoros and Brownsville daily to her job as a shrimp processor and packer. She didn't know how to drive a car, consequently, the family did not own a car. She relied on a neighbor to transport her and other ladies from the neighborhood who worked at the processing plant to shuttle them back and forth every day, for a price of course.

After working in Houston for a time, Eugenio found it difficult to be away from his wife and children. Being away from his wife and children for long periods was not what he had in mind when he moved his family to the southern Texas border.

In 1970, Eugenio decided to look for work closer to home. Some of his friends were shrimpers. They told Eugenio they were earning good money as shrimpers. The work was hard, but the money was better. One of his friends put in a good word for him with his captain. The captain needed another header for the opening of the shrimping season, so, Eugenio got the job. He worked hard, learned fast and two shrimping seasons later, he was promoted to rig man.

Life got better for the Quiñones family. Both parents were working and earning dollars. But they were still living in Mexico (Matamoros). The dream was still, to move to Brownsville, buy a home, enroll the children in school, apply for permanent residency and perhaps even become U.S. citizens. Every time Eugenio came home after a shrimping trip, it was a festive celebration. He had a good paycheck and lots of fish, shrimp, and calamari.

In 1975 after shrimping for five years. Eugenio was now a rig man. It was time to move to Brownsville. He secured a job on the shrimp boat *Rugged but Right*. When he told his shrimping friends that he was going to be the rig man on the *Rugged but Right* captained by Emmett Curtis Amos, his friends advised him against it. Everyone in the shrimping community knew each other.

They know if the owner is a good owner and if the captain treats his crew well. When he signed on to rig on the *Rugged but Right*, he asked the boat owner, Jimmy Russel, for an advance on his pay. He used the money to move the family to Brownsville.

Everyone on the docks he talked to about going shrimping with Captain Emmett Curtis told him not to do it. Emmett Curtis had a bad reputation. He was bad news. He was mean and hard to get along with. He stood over six feet five inches tall and weighed over three hundred pounds.

He was a mean drunk. Every time he came in from shrimping, he got into bar room brawls. Most of the time he was the one who initiated the fights.

Port Isabel/Brownsville shrimping pioneer, captain and owner Charles Burnell, remembers Emmett Curtis well. "He was a bully, a killer." I gave him his first job in shrimping. He came here from Indiana. He had done some jail time up there for stealing tires from a place he worked. He came around the docks looking for work. I was getting ready to go fish down in Campeche and needed another header. He was big, strong and willing to work, so I hired him. I later found out; I had made a mistake bringing him. Campeche trips are long. If you're not used to being out at sea for many days and weeks, it can get to you. Apparently, it got to Emmett Curtis.

"One day, my stepson Steve, who went shrimping with me at times, told Emmett Curtis to go down in the belly hole of the boat and help ice down the shrimp. Emmett told him he wasn't going down in the hole. He was too tired, he wasn't going to do it. Steve told him he was tired too, but the work needed to be done. The shrimp need to be iced as soon as they're headed to keep from spoiling and going bad. Emmett Curtis told Steve he didn't care, he wasn't going to do it. Steve came out of the hole and told Emmett that if he wasn't going to do the job like he was supposed to, he needed to quit and get off the boat when they came back in. They needed men who could handle the job."

"Emmett didn't like the way Steve talked to him. Steve was much smaller and younger than Emmett. He went into a fit of anger and went after Steve, grabbing him by the neck putting him in a choke hold. The other crew members tried to pull Emmett off Steve. They couldn't. Emmett's arms were too powerful. He had Steve in a tight headlock, cutting off his airway. The crew saw Steve was in trouble. He was struggling to get out from the choke hold. Emmett's vise grip around Steve's neck began to stop the air and blood flow to Steve's` head. Seeing this, a crew member ran to the wheelhouse where I was to let me know what was happening. I ran to the stern deck where the men were working. I saw Emmet with his big arms around Steve's neck, strangling him. Steve's arms were no longer flailing. They had fallen listless, dangling, to the sides of his body. His legs had gone limp. He was virtually hanging, almost lifeless, colorless, pale-faced from Emmett's enraged hold. "I'm a big strong man himself. I grabbed Emmett's arms in a desperate attempt to pry Steve loose from him. I pulled, yanked and yelled, as hard as I could. After yelling and yanking at Emmett for what seemed like a long time, he snapped out of his enraged fury. He relaxed his hold on Steve's neck. Steve fell to the deck semiconscious. The other crew members rushed over to Steve and immediately began to shake and fan him trying to get air back into his airway. After he released Steve from his choke hold, I found myself in a face- to-face stare down with the barbarous, crazed giant. I was looking at a man possessed. As scared as I was. I wasn't about to show any weakness. I was the captain and had to show Emmett, who the boss was."

This was not the first-time Charles had confronted an angry crew member in his many years as a captain. But it was the first time he encountered such a monstrosity of a mad man.

"I knew I would be in big trouble if Emmett decided to charge at me, but I stood my ground and was able to talk him down. After that encounter with the crazed Emmett, I told the crew that it was time to end the trip and head for home. We had been out at sea long enough. The news about going home calmed Emmett down."

"As I was getting ready to set course back home, I heard one of my captain friends over the radio broadcast that he was heading home as well. I radioed him and asked him for a favor. I asked him if he would bring Emmett back to Port Brownsville. My friend agreed. We met up a few hours later and Emmett jumped abroad the boat headed for home. I thought it would be best if I got Emmett off my boat. The trip back takes two to three days depending on the weather. Tensions between him and the rest of the crew was still running high. So, to avoid any other fights from breaking out, I sent Emmett back on another boat."

"After I got rid of him. I had a meeting with the remaining crew. We decided to stay in Campeche, to finish the trip. I also did not want to arrive back to port at the same time as Emmett did on the other boat. I didn't want any problems at the dock. I told Emmett I would radio back home and tell my bookkeeper to have his pay ready for him when he got back."

"After getting back to port, Emmett picked up his pay and went on a bar hopping drinking binge. He was heard boasting about what he had done to Steve. He also made it a point to say out loud that Captain Charles had called him "a chicken for doing what he did" to Steve who was much smaller than him. He went on to say that as soon as Captain Charles got back to port, he was going to go looking for him and spit in his face to make him fight. The fight never happened."

Emmett stayed in Brownsville. He got hired by other captains. He learned to shrimp, eventually becoming a captain. Every time he came into port or went into another port up the Gulf Coast, he always managed to get into barroom brawls. He used his gigantic size to beat up other men in the bars. The local police got to know his rowdiness. Every time they were called to a bar where he was fighting, they made sure to bring enough policemen to bring him down.

He liked to dress nicely and always drove a new Lincoln Continental. His ill-tempered reputation got so bad he had a hard time finding crews to fish with him. That's where Eugenio and his friend Antonio Pazos made the mistake of hiring on with him. The start of the 1975 shrimping season was nearing.

Eugenio wanted a job. The *Rugged but Right* needed men.

It was supposed to be a short ten-to-fifteen-day trip. Jimmy Russell, the *Rugged but Right* owner needed a captain for the new season. He hired Emmett. The fifteen-day trip was for Emmett and the crew to familiarize themselves with the boat before the start of the season.

Emmett hired Eugenio and Antonio. He promised to pay them sixteen dollars a box. He also hired Steven Edward Parkklia, a seventeen-year-old runaway from northern Michigan. He had met Parkklia in a bar the night before.

Parkklia told Emmett he was looking for work. Emmett hired him as a header. They sailed out of Brownsville and headed southeast out of Port

Isabel. On the third night Captain Emmett went too close to some underwater rocks. His nets got snagged on the rocks and tore. It took them the rest of the night and half of the next day to put on new nets.

The following night the same thing happened. Emmett, not having learned what happened the night before, trawled close to the rocks again. He repeated his mistake. The nets got caught on the rocks. The boat tilted sharply to one side. They couldn't untangle the nets from the rocks. They had to cut the cables. The nets and the rest of the riggings were lost. They had sunk to the bottom of the Gulf of Mexico.

Murder on the High Seas . . .

According to Steven Parkklia (the seventeen-year-old runaway). Captain Emmett became furious. "He started yelling at Eugenio and Antonio. He blamed them for the snag. Eugenio and Antonio, spoke little English. They tried to explain to Emmett that he was the captain. He was the one who steered the boat too close to the rocks. Getting tangled was his fault.

Emmett angrily told them he was going to cut their pay from sixteen dollars a box to twelve dollars to make up for the loss of rigging and equipment.

Eugenio and Antonio argued back in protest, telling Emmett he was the one who caused the loss of equipment. The argument escalated. More heated words in English and Spanish were exchanged. Captain Emmett left the stern deck in a fury. He went back into the cabin to his bunk. Eugenio and Antonio sat back down to continue heading the shrimp from the drag before.

"A while later Emmett returned yelling and cursing at Eugenio and Antonio. They stood up when they saw him coming. He was still angry yelling at them. He walked up to within a few feet from them, pulled out a pistol, pointed and fired."

"I couldn't believe what was happening! Captain Emmett was completely mad! He shot them both in the gut. They went down grimacing in pain. He came to where I was sitting next to the pile of shrimp and pointed the gun at my head."

(The seventeen-year-old recounted what happened). "I was in total shock. I reacted by diving headfirst into the shrimp pile. I put my hands to the back of my head and started to cry, pleading for my life. Emmett stood over me with the gun pointed at my head. He mumbled some words; I don't remember what. He turned and walked back to the wheelhouse, leaving two men dying on the back deck. I could hear them moaning in pain from the gut shots. I stayed lying face down on the mound of shrimp, crying uncontrollably and paralyzed with fear.

"A few minutes later Emmett returned to the crime scene. By this time, I was able to regain some of my senses. I got up from the pile of shrimp and began to pace back and forth. I didn't know what to do. Eugenio and Antonio were curled in a fetal position holding their stomachs. Their hands were covered in blood. They were in a lot of pain. They were saying something to me in Spanish. I couldn't understand what they were saying. I didn't know what to do. I thought about jumping overboard to escape with my life, but I had no idea where in the middle of the Gulf of Mexico we were. It was dark, all I could see was darkness. There were no other boats in the area. When Emmett came back. I thought for sure he was going to kill me. I began to beg him not to kill me.

"He told me to 'shut the f*** up.' He was not going to kill me. He told me he needed help throwing Eugenio and Antonio over the side into the Gulf waters. After he said that, he went to where Eugenio and Antonio were lying, put the gun to their heads and shot them. He killed them."

"My legs went out from under me. I fell to the deck. I couldn't get up. He yelled at me to stop crying and get up. I couldn't. He pointed the gun at me. I got up. After that I did as he ordered me. I helped him throw Eugenio and Antonio overboard."

"After we threw them over the side, Emmett told me to shovel the rest of the shrimp into the water and wash off the blood from the deck. He went to the wheelhouse. After I cleaned the deck. I stayed back there. I couldn't stop crying. A while later, he yelled at me to come to the wheelhouse. I went. He told me he was taking the boat to Mexico. I pleaded with him not to take me. I wanted to return to the Port of Brownsville. At that point I just wanted off the boat. I told him I would say whatever he wanted me to say to the authorities. Only, not to kill me and take me back."

"After thinking for a while, he decided not to go to Mexico. He told me he was turning the boat around and heading for home. He told me to tell the authorities that the reason he shot and killed Eugenio and Antonio was because they had threatened to kill him, that it was self-defense. I agreed. The four-to-five-hours back to port were the longest, most miserable hours of my life."

"As soon as Captain Emmett got the *Rugged but Right* close enough to the dock to where I could jump from the boat to the dock, I dropped the rope I was holding. I jumped on the dock and ran as fast as I could. I didn`t look back. I ran straight to the highway that was by the docks. I ran towards the direction of Port Isabel. I was able to flag down a car. The man driving the car gave me a ride to town. I asked him to please take me to the police station. I didn`t tell the man in the car why I wanted to go to the police, only that I needed to go there."

By the time Emmett realized Steven had jumped off the boat without tying it to the dock., the boy was out of sight. He couldn`t run to chase him down. He had to position the boat and tie it down himself.

Steven told the police he was a runaway from Michigan. He told them he was hired by Captain Emmett Curtis Amos, as a header on the Rugged but Right. He said there were two other men on board besides him and the captain. They were fishing southeast out of Port Isabel four or five hours out. He told them the captain had killed the two other crew members. He had shot them dead with a pistol.

He told the police the whole story, that the two dead men were Mexicans. He didn't know their full names. He just knew that one was named Eugenio, the other Antonio. He told them he helped the captain throw them overboard because he had to. He was afraid that if he didn't, the captain would kill him too, He explained why the argument started, how Emmett killed them, what happened to Eugenio and Antonio after were they murdered and where they were killed and thrown overboard.

The police, didn`t know whether to believe the runaway's story. He was only seventeen years old. But what he had just told them and the way he recounted it was so sensational that they needed to follow up on it.

This was not the first time Port Isabel police had dealt with murder on the high seas, so they decided to take Steven to where he said the *Rugged but Right* was docked.

Steven told the police he didn`t want to go back to the boat. He was terrified of Emmett. He thought Emmett may still be on the boat. He had a gun and would kill him for sure for betraying him. Besides, he had already told them where the boat was docked. They could find it without him having to come along. The police assured him; they would use caution on approaching the boat. Steven reluctantly agreed to go with the police back to the *Rugged but Right*.

Two police units with four officers went to the Port of Brownsville where Steven said the boat was docked. When they got to the dock, Steven pointed out the boat. He stayed in the car with an officer. The police approached the boat crouching for cover, guns drawn, a safe distance away. They identified themselves as police and called out to the captain of the boat. crouching behind dock pilings at a safe distance. No one answered. They called out again for anyone on the boat to come out. Still no answer.

Port Isabel and Brownsville police are familiar with shrimp boats. Although shrimp boats are not big, there are many places a person can hide without being seen (the cabin, wheelhouse, galley, engine room, the hole, storage bins). They continued to approach with caution, identifying themselves as they went nearer to the boat. They waited a while. No one came out. As they got to the port side of the boat, they noticed that the doors to the cabin and wheelhouse were open.

They boarded, still crouching, still identifying themselves, still calling out to the captain. Still no answer.

Two officers went in through the rear cabin doors and made their way to the wheelhouse, a third officer stayed on the stern deck as back-up. The cabin, galley and wheelhouse had no one in them. They moved to the engine room. No one was in the engine room. They checked the storage bins, no one. They opened the shrimp bins and went down in the hole. No one was there. Emmett was gone. No one was on board.

After securing the boat they begin to look around the back deck. Upon further inspection of the deck, they found blood stains smeared on the deck and railing. Steven had not done a good job of washing off all of Eugenio's and Antonio's blood. They also found some of the fired bullet cartages.

They put a police lockdown on the boat to continue the investigation. They went back to the police car where Steven was waiting. They asked him to give them a full physical description of Captain Emmett. Steven gave it to them.

He also told them he was driving a late-model Lincoln Continental. He wasn't sure of the color. He had only ridden in it once. It was at night; too dark for him to remember the color.

The police notified all other law enforcement agencies to be on the lookout for Emmett. They were advised to proceed with caution if they encountered him. They had reason to believe that he was armed and dangerous. They also contacted the local FBI office. The killings happened in Federal waters, and they needed to be part of the investigation.

After getting off the boat Emmett went on a drinking binge as was his custom. A day later he went back to the Port of Brownsville. He did not, however, go to the boat. He went instead to Jimmy Russell's office. By this time Mr. Russell already knew what had happened. The police had notified him. The only ones who had not yet been notified were the families of the victims, Eugenio Quiñones and Antonio Pazos.

Emmett knew his way around the Port of Brownsville well and was able to avoid being seen by the police guarding the boat.

He sat in Jimmy Russell's office and confessed his crime. According to Captain Charles Burnell, Jimmy Russell's, brother in-law, Jimmy told him Emmett had come to his office the day after his drinking spree. He was drunk and distressed. At one point during his visit with Mr. Russell, Emmett broke down crying. He crouched over on the chair he was sitting in put his face in his hands and began to sob.

Emmett admitted the murders. Jimmy Russell told him the police were looking for him. He needed to turn himself in. He left Jimmy's office and drove off. He drove his Lincoln towards Brownsville on Highway 48. He pulled over to the side of the road, got out of his car to throw up the alcoholic contents in his stomach. A sheriff's deputy on patrol saw him. He radioed dispatch that he was turning around to investigate. Another deputy on patrol heard the radio communication and drove to the location to assist.

The radio report to dispatch was of a man who was on the side of the road throwing up. The deputies questioned him. He was given a field sobriety test. He failed. He was placed under arrest.

Placing Emmett under arrest was the easy part. Handcuffing him and putting him in the patrol unit was a whole other matter. The six foot five-inch-tall, three-hundred-pound Emmett resisted. He had been in many scuffles with the police before. All for fighting and disorderly conduct. He wasn't afraid of the police nor did he respect their authority. Fisticuffs broke out. Somehow the deputies were able to subdue him, put him in the patrol car and transport him to the county jail where they booked him for a DWI.

The sheriff's office knew who they had in custody. Emmett Curtis Amos had been in their jail several times before. They did not know at the time of his booking that he was wanted on suspicion of murdering two of his crew members on the high seas.

They found out the following day when the FBI contacted them to be on the lookout for Emmett Curtis Amos for questioning in the murders. They warned the sheriff to approach with caution. Emmett was armed and dangerous. The sheriff informed the FBI they had him in their jail. They had arrested him the day before for a DWI. The FBI immediately went to the county jail and placed him in their custody. He was taken before the Federal Magistrate, Judge William Mallett, for arraignment. He was charged with murder on the high seas. His bond was set at $75,000. He continued to gloat and self-gratify himself behind his jail cell bars. He bragged about the murders. He told the jail guards and other prisoners about how he had killed two Mexicans.

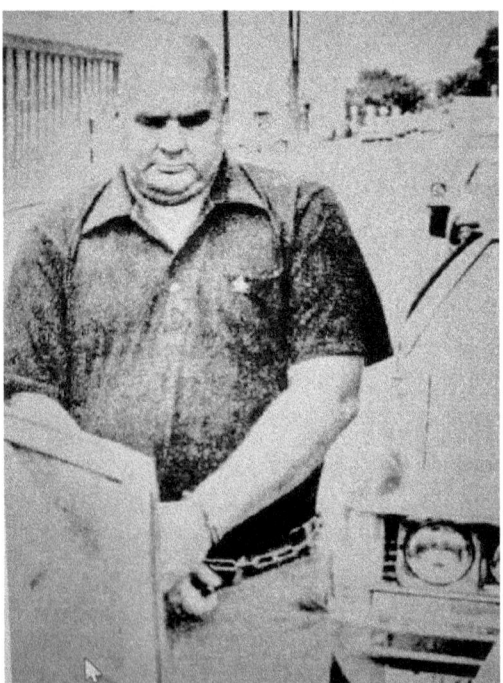

Captain Emmett Curtis Amos after arraignment

Steve Parkklia, the only witness to the murders, was never detained by the police or FBI. They took his statement, followed by investigating and gathering the evidence on the *Rugged but Right*. Satisfied that he was telling the truth and that he had no part in the murders, they told him he was free to go about his business.

He hung around Port Isabel/Brownsville for about week. He waited for some money his parents sent to him for the bus ride back home.

During the week that he was waiting for money from home, he hung around the Port of Brownsville shrimp docks. He became a minor celebrity among the local shrimpers. During one of those days of walking the docks, he spoke to Captain Charles Burnell. He recounted the same murderous story he had told the police.

He told Captain Burnell he was a runaway and how he met Emmett Curtis Amos, in a Brownsville bar. He said he was hired as a header, going shrimping on the *Rugged but Right* and witnessing the murders.

After he received the money from his parents to return home, he left and never returned to Texas.

Steven Parkklia presently lives in Wisconsin. I interviewed Steven by telephone. He told me that for many years, he was haunted by the tragic murders of Eugenio and Antonio. He remembered Eugenio and Antonio as good, friendly men. "They treated me well. They took good care of me. They taught me how to work on the boat. They spoke little English," he said. "I spoke no Spanish at all." He remembered how they had fun teaching each other English and Spanish.

Parkklia recalled the night of the murders. "I felt bad for the families of Eugenio and Antonio. They didn't do anything wrong. It was Captain Emmett who put us on the rocks. He was the one who went crazy and murdered them. After I left Brownsville, I never went back to Texas. The nightmarish experience haunted me for years. I never spoke to the families. I didn't know where to get ahold of them. I never knew if the bodies were ever found. In truth, I just wanted to put the whole ordeal behind me."

The Eugenio Quiñones Family . . .

The Quiñones were living on 26th Street in the Southmost neighborhood of Brownsville. They were happy. After years of taking one day at a time, they had finally done it.

It was a rental, nothing fancy. Three bedrooms, one bath, no closets. The house was just a wood frame shell dwelling. But the family didn`t care. They had lived in worse conditions. They were going to convert the house into a happy home. The school age children were enrolled in school. Dad was shrimping. He was going to earn lots of money. Their prospects for prosperity were getting brighter.

One of the last things Eugenio told his wife Maria Elena, before he left to fish on the *Rugged but Right* was that no matter what happened to him, she had to promise him that she was going to make sure the children studied hard, stayed in school and got a good education.

He told her this not because he felt he was not going to return home after the shrimping trip. He told her that because he understood how dangerous a job shrimping is.

Six days after Eugenio, Sr. left on what happened to be his final and fatal shrimping trip, the local television news broadcasted the story about the murders of some shrimpers on the high seas. Nine-year-old Magda Quiñones saw the report. They showed a picture of one of the victims. It looked exactly like her father.

She didn't speak or understand English well. The only thing she was able to make sense of during the broadcast was the name Enrique Quiñones. The news reporter on the TV kept saying the name Enrique, instead of Eugenio. She was confused, not knowing what to think. She wondered who the man being called Enrique, that looked exactly like her father was and why was the newsman talking about him.

It took the local police and the FBI a couple of days to find the Quiñones family. They started looking for them in colonia Modelo, Matamoros, Mexico. their former place of residence before they moved to Brownsville. The neighbors there told them the family had moved to Brownsville. Somehow the FBI, was able to find Maria Elena's mother. They informed her of what had happened to Eugenio and that they needed to let Maria Elena know. She took them to their new address.

Eugenio Quiñones Jr. remembers the day his maternal grandmother walked up to the house accompanied by the two FBI agents. "We were in the living room trying to make sense of what our sister Magda had just seen and heard on the television news. They noticed that an official-looking government car had parked on the street in front of our house. We saw our grandmother walking with the agents up the walkway towards the front door. Mother went out to meet them. She told us kids to wait inside. We stood at the doorway looking at our mother as she walked to meet the agents. The words exchanged between Mother and the FBI agents weren't that many. They said something I don't know what. Our grandmother said something to our mom too. As soon as our grandmother said what she said, we heard the most agonizing scream come from our mother. The cry was so piercing that it startled us. All of us immediately began to tremble where we stood. We started asking each other what was happening.

We saw Mother drop to the ground. Grandmother tried to hold her up, but her limp body was too heavy. She began to roll on the ground crying, yelling, the word 'no' over and over. Neighbors started to come out to their front yards, others looked out the windows and front doors of their homes, everyone who had heard Mom`s scream wanted to know what was going on at our house." The six Quiñones children, ranging from ages nine years to three months, stood at the front door shaking and confused. They didn`t understand what was happening. The sight of their mother rolling on the ground sobbing horrified them. Never had they seen their mother in such emotional pain. They didn`t know how to help her at that moment.

"I had just turned five years old two days before. The twins were three months old; Adriana was seven and Magda nine. We were just kids."

The twins Perla and Esmeralda have no memory of their father or the murderous tragedy. All they know of him is what they have been told by their older siblings and their mother. To this day, forty-seven years later, they still grieve his death. They know who he was from the many stories their mother and siblings have told them. They know what he looked like from photographs.

They still feel overcome with emotion when the family speaks of him. Knowing that they were three months old when their father died allows them to understand what they have been told that their father lovingly cradled them in his arms and loved them. They know with certainty that they did hear his words of love.

For days after the heartbreaking news the Quiñones family grieved the loss of their father. Maria Elena held on to him by hugging his dress suit, that hung on a coat hanger nailed to their bedroom wall. The smell of his cologne imbedded in the suit kept her going back to it. The initial denial of his death was replaced by hope that by some miracle, he may have survived his gunshot wounds and swam to some beach somewhere.

She hoped that he would recover his health and eventually find his way back home.

For years Maria Elena continued to hope and pray for her husband`s return. She could not fully accept the reality that he was never returning. Her other hope was that if he in fact was dead, that his body be recovered and returned to her. This way she and the children could give him a proper Christian funeral. They needed closure from their tragic loss. Their grieving went from disbelief, to anger, sadness, longing, thoughts and memories of him.

The Quiñones family continues to mourn his life to this day. Every year on the anniversary of his death, the family brings a floral gift to the jetties of South Padre Island. They toss the flowers into the waters of the Gulf of Mexico and have a prayer service for him.

After recovering from the shock of her husband's murder, Maria Elena took on an unwavering, resolute and determined focus of her energies on the welfare and wellbeing of her children. She was a devout believer in God and knew that for them to survive and move on with their lives in a productive way, she needed to make sure that she and her children continue to grow spiritually. She was going to shepherd them from gloom and despair to light and resilience.

It was up to her to raise the children with proper guidance. The lack of a father was not going to be an excuse or reason for the children to become delinquent in their studies or make bad behavior choices. She got them involved in their parish. They all became altar servers. All five of her daughters were crowned parish queens. The annual coronation honor of parish queen always went to the young Miss who raised the most money for the church during the bazaar. Maria Elena didn't have out of pocket money to contribute towards her daughter's cash totals so she worked hard at the laborious task of making and selling tamales.

She always kept Eugenio's expectations for the children alive. Every one of them excelled in school. They graduated from high school and college earning advanced graduate degrees. The girls became teachers and school administrators. Eugenio Jr. is a supervisor with the U.S. Border Patrol.

After Eugenio's death, the in-laws on his side of the family took a more pessimistic attitude towards Maria Elena's ability to successfully raise the children on her own. They suggested that she move back to Monterrey, Mexico, with the children. The U.S. was not a good place for her to bring up the children. Maria Elena stood her ground. She told them Eugenio made her promise to raise the children in the U.S. regardless of whatever happened to him.

They immigrated to the U.S. with little money. But he understood that with hard work and perseverance they were going to make this the land of opportunity for them. There was no going back, only forward.

She stayed true to her word. She worked her fingers to the bone. She headed and packed shrimp in the fish houses, she worked as a domestic housekeeper, cleaning other people's houses as well as raising their children. She sorted and stuffed for the *Bargain Book*, a weekly newspaper circular that advertised all types of product sales at bargain prices.

She never sought companionship with another man. Eugenio was her only true love. The only man she was ever with.

They didn't forget their beloved Mexico. They never forgot where they came from. Culturally, they evolved from Mexicans to Mexican Americans.

Once a year they made their annual trip to visit family in Mexico. The kids loved it. They got to reconnect with grandparents, aunts, uncles, cousins. The extended family in Mexico loved their visits as well. Every year Maria Elena saved as much money as she could for the trip. They never traveled there with just their clothes and luggage. They brought with them gifts, as well as household items she knew their relatives in Mexico needed.

They were a mini caravan. Each child was packed and loaded down, not only with their personal belongings for the trip but all the rest of the gifts they were bringing. They walked single file across the International Bridge from Brownville to Matamoros, one behind the other with Maria Elena leading the way. Each hand carried a bag filled with items. When they got to the Mexican side, they took a city bus to the central bus terminal deep inside of Matamoros. At the central bus terminal, they took the bigger transport bus for the trip to Monterrey.

The Killer goes to Trial . . .

The *United States of America vs. Emmett Curtis Amos*. The charge: two counts of murder on the high seas. The penalty: Death or Life Imprisonment on each count. The plea: Not Guilty. The trial was set for 16 June 1975.

Four days later the killer returned to court with court-appointed attorney Juan E. Gavito. Judge O'Connor ordered Emmett be sent to a psychiatric hospital in Springfield, Missouri, for examination. Three months after that, Judge O'Connor set the jury trial for 07 October 1975.

On the day of his trial, Emmett appeared before the judge. pleading guilty to two counts of voluntary manslaughter. Apparently, after some plea bargaining between his court-appointed public defense attorney, the

United States attorneys and the judge, they struck a deal. He was sentenced to ten years on each count, one and two to run concurrently. The killer, now guilty, did not go to prison. He was committed to a psychiatric institution where he could receive psychiatric treatment.

After weighing his options. Emmett decided against a jury trial. If found guilty of murder, he was going to be put to death or spend the rest of his life in prison. So, he took the gravy train trip to the psychiatric hospital instead.

There he would have time (ten years) to con and convince his treating psychiatrists, that they were so skilled and good in their psychiatric treatment methods that they were able to cure him of his criminally insane sociopathic personality.

His strategy worked. Within a matter of a few years and no time in prison, Emmett was back in Brownsville. The psychiatrists who treated him told the court he was cured. They said he was no longer a threat to society. He was released with time served in the psychiatric institution.

A few years later he was back in Brownsville. Not as a shrimper. No one in the shrimping industry wanted anything to do with him. He got involved in transporting marijuana up north.

According to some people, he made lots of money. He liked to drive Lincoln Continentals. He loaded his Lincoln with weed and drove it to the immigration check point at Sarita. The Border Patrol agents asked him if he was a U.S. citizen. He answered yes and he was waved on by. It was during the 1980s and the U.S. Customs & Border Patrol drug sniffing dog program was not as advanced as it is today.

Emmitt bragged that when he came to the inspection check point, the Border Patrol agents saw a neatly dressed white guy in a nice shiny car. They let him pass. He was eventually caught, tried and convicted for transporting drugs and sent to prison. It wasn't Border Patrol or Customs who busted him. Ironically, he had pulled over to the side of a highway with car trouble somewhere near Port Arthur, Texas. A local police patrol stopped to check on him. Upon further inspection of his car, the police officer found a load of marijuana.

He was never heard of or seen in the Brownsville area again after that.

Maria Elena and the children went on to put their lives back in order as best as they could. She instilled in them good family values. She made sure never to come across as weak, no matter how difficult the challenge facing them. They did everything together. They went everywhere together. When they went to church, Maria Elena led the way. When they went to the grocery store for their weekly shopping, they all went. They didn't have a car, so they walked to and from everywhere no matter how cold or hot the day.

Walking to the store was the easy part. The walk back was the work part of the outing. Each one of the children was responsible for toting their share of the groceries. The older ones carried the heavy items like the twenty-five-pound sack of flour for tortillas, the five pounds of pinto beans and rice, as well as the five-pound bucket of lard used for tortillas and cooking. The smaller children carried the lighter bundles, stopping several times along the way to rest.

When Magda and Adriana turned into young teens, they earned money by babysitting for family, friends and neighbors.

Eugenio, Jr. was eight years old when he went to work for Mr. Rosenbaum, a grocer and pioneer businessman in the southernmost neighborhood of Brownsville. At three o' clock when school let out, he ran home, ate a tortilla with butter, then ran to Rosenbaum's to sack groceries, sweep, and do whatever Mr. Rosenbaum needed him to do until 9:00 p.m. closing time.

At sixteen, Magda got a summer job working for *Manpower*, a federally funded program that helped with job training and placement. She saved as much of her money earned as she could. At the end of summer, she took what she had saved and bought a used car. When she showed up at the house proud as could be with her brand-new used car, her mother questioned. "Magda, why did you go and spend your money on a car? You don't even know how to drive." Magda, replied, "That's true, Mama, but I will learn. It is my money that I saved, and this is our car. From now on we will never have to walk anywhere or ask anyone for a ride ever again."

Maria Elena bought the house on 26th Street. She sued the boat, *Rugged but Right*. It wasn't a huge settlement but it was enough to pay for the house. The rest of the money she put in the bank. The money however didn't stay in the bank for long. When she went to the bank to deposit the remaining money, a woman named "Bidi" Ramirez, who worked there befriended her and helped her open a savings account. Every time Maria Elena went to the bank to deposit money in her savings, the Ramirez woman went out of her way to attend to her banking needs. One-day Bidi and her husband Arturo Ramirez, a Brownsville, police officer visited Maria Elena, at her house.

The Ramirez's knew where Maria Elena lived from her bank records. They asked her for a personal loan. It was going to be a short-term loan of only a few weeks. They told Maria Elena they were expecting some money soon. As soon as the money came, they would pay her back with interest of course.

Maria Elena agreed to loan them the money. Bidi had been nice to her, she worked at the bank. Arturo was a police officer. Never did she think he would take her money and not pay her back.

The loan repayment went from weeks, to months, to years, to never.

She was conned, scammed and robbed by the Ramirez's. A crooked cop and a thieving banker.

She still owns the house on 26th Street. She now lives with her son Eugenio, Jr. The family keeps the house as a testament to the seed of a dream she and Eugenio planted there all those many years ago. The seeded dream that took root and sprouted despite tragedy and adversity. Maria Elena was widowed at thirty-one years of age. She never remarried. She dedicated her entire life to God, who in return blessed her with the strength to keep the family together. She prioritized the children's health, welfare and education, placing all their needs before hers and she kept Eugenio's American dream legacy alive.

Maria Elena is proud that she was a shrimper's wife. She knew then and understands today that the job of a shrimper is a dangerous one. Accidents occur out at sea that result in serious injury and sadly, death at times. But no shrimper wife ever expects that the death of her husband will be caused by the crazed mind of a sadistic captain.

Shrimper wives are clear in knowing that the lives and safety of a captain's crew is his number one priority above anything else. They fully expect that from the moment the boat leaves the dock to the moment the boat ties back again at the end of the trip, that the captain will return their husbands back safe and sound.

It's tragic enough to lose a husband at sea because of an accident. It's worse for the captain to murder him in cold blood, throw the body overboard for the sharks to eat, never to be seen again.

Maria Elena's consolation today is knowing that Eugenio is spiritually present with her. She has felt this ever since his death. She, the children, the grandchildren and all other Quinñones, who will follow shall know of his presence, every time they visit the Cristo de Los Pescadores where he and all other shrimpers from Port Isabel and Brownsville who have died at sea shall forever be memorialized.

Rest in Peace Eugenio. Peace be with you, Maria Elena, Magda, Adriana, Eugenio Jr, Esmeralda, Perla, Maria Elena (daughter).

27

LUPITA VILLARREAL

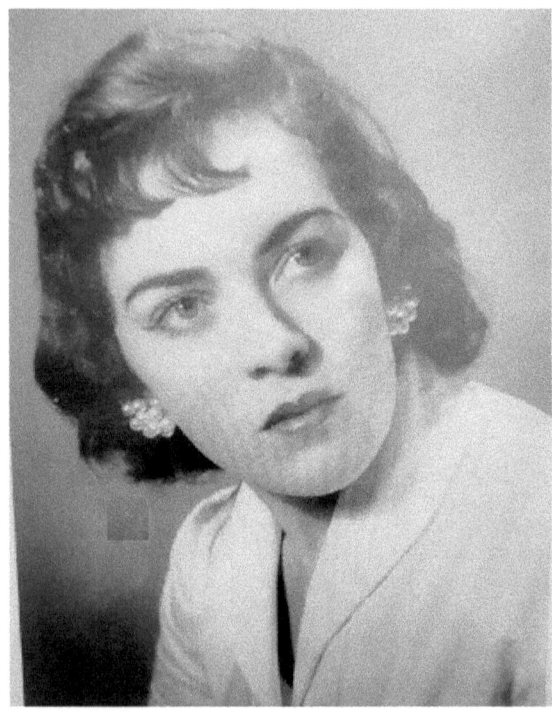

More than sixty years ago, Lupita married her high school sweetheart, Sabino Villarreal. Together they raised a son Rene and spent their lives working in the Port Isabel shrimping industry. Their story is one of dreams, success, loss and endurance.

Lupita spent eighteen years working at *WBP* (White, Brown and Pink shrimp fish house) before she became a full-time co-owner of three shrimp boats.

Martin Tower owned the *WBP* company, and his daughter Margie managed the office. She had grown up in the industry and knew all aspects of the business.

"Margie was an excellent boss and manager. She treated everyone well. She did all the hiring of the crew and developed strong relationships with them," Lupita told us.

"I remember one time a boy had gotten seasick. Days passed and he had not gotten over the sea sickness. He vomited for days, became dehydrated and became dangerously ill. The captain didn't have a choice. He had to bring him back. Luckily, the boy recovered after a few days. Margie handled the incident with her usual calmness. Her main concern was the boy's health."

"I think that women, especially Margie, had more and better communication with the crew. I learned a lot about building relationships with the crew from her."

When Margie passed away, her stepmother Leonor took over managing the boats. Lupita became office manager and she assumed responsibility for keeping the books, ordering supplies, negotiating the bidding and purchase price of shrimp with the buyers, issuing settlement statements with the crew, and other office duties.

"Working for the Towers was a good experience," Lupita said. "I met a lot of the family, and they were all friendly and nice."

"Once Sabino and I bought our first boat, I set up an office in the back of our house and managed both jobs at once. I stayed with *WBP* until they brought in more family members and then they laid me off."

Lupita and Sabino were boat owners for fifteen years. Their first boat, the *Rene Boy*, named after their son, became the cornerstone for building their fleet to three boats. Together they enjoyed the good times and profitable years as well as the pride of being boat owners and living their dream. They bought a bigger house with a swimming pool in a nice neighborhood, they drove nice cars, took nice family vacations and built up their savings accounts towards retirement.

"It was the happiest time of our lives," Sabino told us. "We achieved our goal and loved working in the business. Lupita was a hands-on owner. She managed all the money as well as maintenance and repairs of the boats. Shrimp boat supplies, electrical instrumentations, rigging and engine repairs are expensive.

The Gulf of Mexico is brutal on boats. They take a non-stop battering from the moment they clear the jetties, until they come back in again. Gulf trawling shrimp boats are considered small vessels out on the vast open seas of the Gulf of Mexico.

Crew members can be negligent with their care of the boat. It doesn't belong to them and none of the repairs cost them any money. They are paid their share regardless. The money that's left over after taking their cut must be used for maintenance and operation of the boat. What inattentive captains don't realize or perhaps don't care is that if they do not do their best to take good care of the boat, it will affect their earnings in the long run.

When the paychecks get smaller because the boat keeps coming in for repairs, the captain and crew will quit and get off the boat. The problem with that is that when the captain goes to another fish house to ask for a job, the owner he asks for a job will call the previous owner and ask about him. Rest assure that his former boss will without hesitation give him a bad reference.

Everyone in the shrimping world knows about one another. Word spreads fast in shrimping. Good rig men and headers will not go fishing with a bad captain. There is no money in it for them. Shrimpers fish to make money. From owners to captains to rig men to headers, it's all about the money.

Lupita and Sabino were doing well. They were making money.

Then in the 1980s the bad times hit.

Piracy on the High Seas . . .

Two of their boats, the *Miss Lupita* and the *Christy Crystal* were seized on the same day by the Mexican government for ostensibly fishing in Mexican waters. The *Miss Lupita* was anchored in international waters, the *Christy Crystal*, was running deeper into Mexican waters.

Sabino knows this because he was notified by the U.S. Coast Guard that his boats were being seized. After the seizure, the captain in command of the Coast Guard Station at Brazos asked Sabino to meet him and some of his staff at the Holiday Inn Hotel on South Padre Island. Sabino thought the meeting place was out of the ordinary. Nonetheless, he went to the Holiday Inn.

"After we received the call from the Coast Guard, we immediately contacted U.S. Congressman Solomon Ortiz, who told us to go to the meeting with the Coast Guard. They showed us a video tape that showed where *Miss Lupita* was anchored. Her coordinates verified she was in international waters. They also showed us in the tape where the *Christy Crystal* was headed towards Mexico. We talked to our lawyer to discuss and plan to go to Tampico, Mexico so we could get our boats back. The next day we called the Coast Guard to ask for a copy of the video they had shown us the day before. They told us they no longer had the video in their possession. They had sent it further up the chain of command to another station, but they never told us where."

"Congressman Solomon Ortiz was no help either. At the time when our boats were taken by the Mexican Navy, the U.S. was working on the Free Trade Agreement with Mexico and Canada. Congressman Ortiz did not want what appeared to be the piracy of our boats to become an international incident between Mexico and the U.S. There was much more at stake than our two little boats. He turned his back on us."

"The two captains of our boats were friends. One went by the nickname of Patos (Ducks), the other by the nickname of La Calavera (The Skull). They had strict orders from us not to fish Mexican waters." La Calavera was a Mexican national with U.S. work papers. As we began to investigate and connect the dots of how things happened, we suspected that the seizure of our boats was a planned deal between our captains and the Mexican Navy captain and who knows who else in Tampico."

Being from Mexico, La Calavera had ties and contacts over there. An interesting thing happened after they were apprehended and taken to

Tampico. They and the crew were released right away. That hardly ever happens. Usually when U.S. boats are caught fishing in Mexican waters and taken to Tampico there is some kind of detainment, a hearing, charges and hefty fines paid before the crew is released.

That didn't happen in the case of the crews for the *Miss Lupita* and the *Christy Crystal*. The crews were back in the U.S. before Sabino even got to Tampico. They could have passed each other on the road. Sabino was going to Tampico and the crew members were coming to the U.S.

Before Sabino left Port Isabel to go to Tampico, he had met with his lawyer Denis Sanchez, who had contacted a Mexican lawyer in Tampico. Sanchez asked Sabino for $10,000. He sent the money to the lawyer in Tampico and gave Sabino the name and address of his office there. When Sabino went to the lawyer's office in Tampico, he was told that the lawyer was not in. Sabino went to the Port of Tampico to look for his boats. He identified himself as the owner of the *Miss Lupita* and *Christy Crystal* and wanted to speak with the person in command about his boats. The Mexican Navy sailors on guard did not let him pass the perimeter they were guarding. They told him they would relay his request to the Navy officer in command known as the Captain of the Port. When Sabino asked the guards if his boats were there, they wouldn't tell him, only that he should come back later.

He went back to the lawyer's office. The lawyer wasn't there. This went on for five days. On the fifth day, the Captain of the Port finally agreed to meet with Sabino. He told Sabino that his boats were seized because they were caught fishing in Mexican waters illegally. Sabino stated his case. He told the Captain of the Port that the U.S. Coast Guard told him that yes, the *Christy Crystal*, was in Mexican waters but was not fishing. He said that the U.S. Coast Guard also showed him evidence that the *Miss Lupita* was anchored out in international waters when she was taken into custody by the Mexican Navy.

The Captain of the Port told Sabino that he had no evidence of that. As far as the Mexican government is concerned both boats were fishing in Mexican waters illegally. When Sabino asked how much money it was going to take to get his boats back, he was told it was going to cost him more than $100,000.

Again, Sabino went looking for the lawyer who had been paid his $10,000. The lawyer again was not there. By this time Sabino, who is a diabetic, had run out of insulin. He began to feel sick. He had to return to Port Isabel. When he got back home, he was so sick that he had to be taken to the Veterans hospital in San Antonio, Texas. The lack of insulin and the stress he went through in Tampico almost killed him. The entire incident was a horrible nightmare that to this day they have not been able to recover from. They were victimized by two unscrupulous captains. Soon after the incidents, the same two captains came up with enough money to buy shrimp boats of their own.

None of the *Miss Lupita* and *Christy Crystal* crew members were ever questioned by U.S. authorities when they came back from Mexico. As far as they were concerned Sabino's and Lupita's boat problem was between them and Mexico. The boats were lost, taken by the Mexican government. Lupita and Sabino didn't have the kind of cash they needed to pay off the Mexican government to bring them back. Besides the thousands of dollars it would take to pay for their release, they would have to spend many thousands more equipping and rigging them again.

Sabino and Lupita were still licking their wounds from their losses when a couple of weeks later, lo and behold...here comes the *Christy Crystal* sputtering back home to Port Isabel. It docked at *Zimco Marine*. Apparently, it came in with mechanical problems and had become disabled at sea. Port Isabel was closer to them than their now home port of Tampico, so the Mexican captain radioed the U.S. Coast Guard with their distress, and he was allowed to bring the boat in for repairs.

There is a maritime law and agreement between countries that whenever a foreign marine vessel is in distress or needs safe harbor from a storm they can go into the nearest port for repair or shelter.

When Lupita and Sabino were told by other shrimper friends that the *Christy Crystal* was tied up at *Zimco*, they rushed right over to the dock. They couldn't believe their eyes. It was their darling *Christy Crystal*. She was worn, battered and broken but it was her. They had her back. They could hardly control their excitement. They thought they had lost her forever. The joy and happiness they felt was short lived.

"We went to the authorities, hoping to get our boat back. We showed them our papers of ownership and asked them for help in taking back possession of the boat, but we got no cooperation. Law enforcement sided with and protected the Mexicans. They said the boat belonged to Mexico. The authorities told me straight out that if I tried to board the boat, to take it back I would be arrested. To make matters worse, the sheriff ordered some of his deputies to stand guard and not let me get near our *Christy Crystal*. We almost went crazy! You can only imagine the anguish we were going through.

Having to stand a mere rock's throw away from our boat. Seeing the Mexican crew on board, leisurely relaxing laughing, lounging, listening to music. They ran out of groceries, so the authorities brought them groceries. They allowed mechanics and other repairmen to board her and make repairs. They did all these crazy things under our government's protection.

"Lupita and I were the bad guys. They, the foreigners who had committed piracy, on us by stealing our boats were the good guys.

"Every U.S. government agency we went to for help refused us. They rejected us. I am an army veteran. I served our country. We couldn't comprehend why we were being treated this way. The authorities kept telling us they could not get involved because the crew had not broken any U.S. laws. The boat had become disabled. The captain asked for permission to seek safe harbor and come in for repairs. International Maritime protocol allows foreign sea vessels to enter a foreign port for safe harbor or repairs.

"If they ordered the crew off the boat so that we could take it back, they could be accused of participating in something that could cause and international incident against Mexico and her people."

Lupita still finds it difficult to talk about the loss. It's a bad memory impossible to remit to the vault of her mind. They had one boat left The *Rene Boy*, their flagship boat. It was a great source of pride.

It was the *Rene Boy* who first began to earn money for them. Like all successful businesses. To keep the business going and make it grow, you must put money back into it. They did and that's how they were able to acquire the *Miss Lupita* and later the *Christy Crystal*. They were on their way to building a small fleet of shrimp boats, when their misfortune happened.

Still reeling from the loss of two of their boats. Bad luck wasn't done with Lupita and Sabino yet. They say you shouldn't kick a person when they're down. As Lupita and Sabino licked their wounds, they regrouped and focused on the *Rene Boy*. They were going to rebuild the fleet. They were going to work hard, save money and buy more boats. They had done it before; they could do it again.

They still held on to the dream. The nightmare was in the past. They were going to pick themselves up, dust themselves off and start over.

Easier said than done. it didn't happen as they planned. No sooner had they begun to save money again with the *Rene Boy* when a group of other local shrimp boat fleet owners, along with lawyer Dennis Sanchez, formed a cooperation, which worked out a deal with the SBA (Small Business Association). They negotiated a dollar amount and bought up a slew of independent SBA shrimp boat loans. Most of the loans were mortgaged to small one boat owners, trying to make a living and support their families. The *Rene Boy* was one of those boats.

At first, the small independent boat owners were fine with the SBA selling their mortgages to the local cooperation of larger fleet owners. They all knew each other. They did business with one another. They lived in the same community. As far as the small independents knew, it was going to be business as usual.

They never thought friends or as they found out, not friends at all, would stab them in the gut. They called the loans. They told the independents they must pay the note in full or forfeit the boat. Lupita and Sabino owed $24,000. They didn't have the money. All their money had been spent paying lawyers trying to get their boats back. Most of the others didn't have the money either. The boats were repossessed.

Lupita and Sabino had no more boats. Two were stolen as far as they're concerned, the other taken by greedy people they thought were friends.

To make matters worse, pouring salt on the wound, the cooperation decided they had no use for the boats. They didn't want to bother with them. They sold them to a salvage company for scrap. The independents stood on the dock and watched as their family's means of support were dismantled and torn apart piece by piece, hauled away and sold as scrap.

Despite the hardship of bad times. Lupita fondly remembers the best of times. "For years, we had no major problems and the hauls of shrimp were always good. It was a special time."

"Every year at the beginning of the season, every boat selected a princess candidate, to be crowned that year's Shrimp Fiesta queen. We all gave a donation to Our Lady Star of the Sea Catholic Church to take part in the festivities. On the evening of July 15, the boats all sailed through the jetties into the Gulf waters."

"When the boats came in the families went to the docks to head shrimp, unload and process the catch. They were great years. Those were the years of the ice boats. Refrigeration came in during the 1970s."

"The best of times," Sabino agreed. "I loved the life of being a boat owner. I didn't like going out on the boat and fishing for shrimp. I got seasick!"

Their love for one another has pulled them through all these rough times and they fondly reminisce of their golden days in shrimping.

28

HANDS

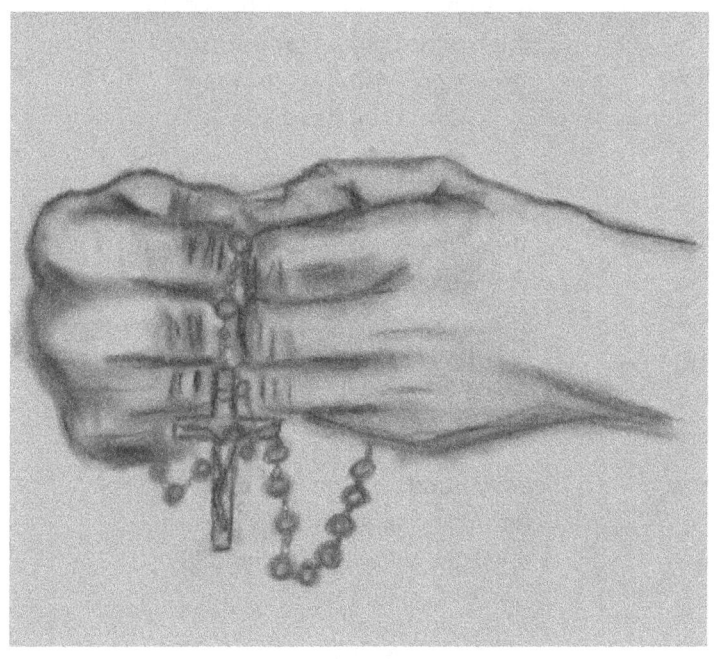

See my hands, so big and cracked
Swollen fingers, broken, bent
Rope burnt fossils mixed with prints
Joined together...

In silent prayer

See these hands that venture deep
To the bottom of the sea
Scraped and bruised from heaves and hoes
Cross the torso...

In silent prayer

See my hands so strong yet torn
By bewildered creatures that they
Trawled up
Flip the pages...

In silent prayer

See these hands that chart the course
To the next excursion far out to sea
Knowing not what waits ahead
Count the beads...

In silent prayer

See these hands so wet and chapped
Steer the vessel through tempest storm.
Wipe the brow
Relight the candle...

In silent prayer

See my hands so washed, so clean
Returning safely from the sea
Caress the wife, embracing tight
Consummate...

In silent prayer

See these hands so coarse yet gentle
Tenderly cradle the little children
Lifting them skyward
Beholding God...

In silent prayer

See my hands so skilled that built
A home on land from life at sea
Dip the fingers into holy water
Wave the blessed palms with them...

In silent prayer

See these hands crustaceous red
One holds wife, the other holds child
Joyous and faithful are we three
Kneel in church...

In silent prayer

See my hands so big, so cracked
Swollen fingers, broken, bent
Wave Adios from trawler's deck
To wife with child
Cross the torso with the beads...

In silent prayer
Amen

www.ingramcontent.com/pod-product-compliance
Lightning Source LLC
Chambersburg PA
CBHW071004160426
43193CB00012B/1908